NTS
GW01607635

Published by Core 1WML Limited
Windmill Lane
Dublin
Ireland
D02 F206

www.onecore.ie

First printed 2017
Reprinted 2021

ISBN: 978-1-7398239-1-7

Designed and typeset by www.sandbox.ie

Part one of this book ("the Study") has been written by Jim Power Economics Limited for Core 1WML Limited ("Core") and the Association of Advertisers in Ireland ("the AAI"). Part two of the Study was written by Core.

The Study has been prepared for the purpose of surveying the global literature covering the relationships between marketing communications, macroeconomics and microeconomics. It should not be used for any other purpose or in any other context. Jim Power Economics Limited, Core and the AAI accept no responsibility for its use by any party for decision making or reporting to third parties or any other purpose.

No party other than Core and the AAI is entitled to rely on the Study for any purpose whatsoever and Jim Power Economics Limited, Core and the AAI accept no responsibility or liability or duty of care to any party in respect of the Study or any of its contents.

The information contained in the Study has been obtained from Core and third party sources that are clearly referenced in the appropriate sections of the Study. Jim Power Economics Limited, Core and the AAI have neither sought to corroborate this information nor to review its overall reasonableness.

Accordingly, no representation or warranty of any nature, either express or implied, is given and no responsibility or liability is or will be accepted by or on behalf of Jim Power Economics Limited, Core and the AAI as to the accuracy, completeness or correctness of the information contained in this book and any such liability is expressly disclaimed.

Jim Power Economics Limited, Core and the AAI disclaim any liability arising out of the use of the Study and its contents, including any action or decision taken as a result of such use.

ABOUT THE AUTHORS

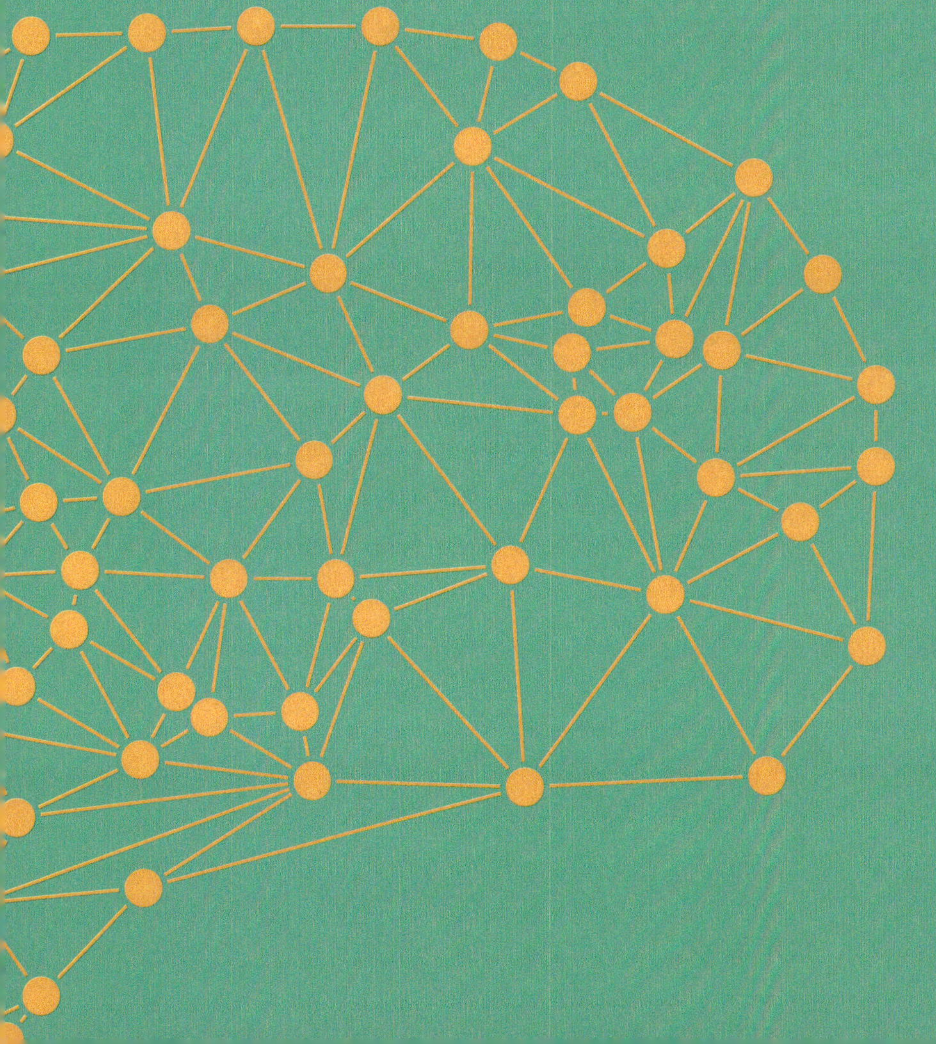

CHRIS JOHNS

Chris Johns is a founder of Rumney Consulting and a co-founder of CJP Consultants. Both companies carry out consultancy projects, public speaking and training for a variety of public and private sector entities.

He has worked in financial services, mostly asset management and investment banking, since 1986. His most recent role was Chief Investment Officer for global fundamental equities with State Street Global Advisers (SSgA). Prior to that he was CEO and CIO (Chief Investment Officer) at Bank of Ireland Asset Management until the sale of that business to SSgA.

As a member of the SSgA Executive Management Team, Chris led the business through the transition to new ownership, successfully integrating the firm while continuing to manage the equity investment management business.

Chris also worked as an economist in the UK Treasury, the National Institute of Economic & Social Research and UBS Phillips & Drew in London, while also teaching economics in London and Cambridge Universities.

Originally from Cardiff, Chris was a member of the Welsh Assembly Government's Economic Research Advisory panel between 2002 and 2012.

Chris is a regular columnist with The Irish Times and wrote the 'London Briefing' and 'Serious Money' columns for the newspaper from 2002 until 2006.

JIM POWER

Jim Power is owner manager of Jim Power Economics Limited, an economic and financial consultancy. In 2013, he co-founded CJP Consultants with Chris Johns. Both companies carry out consultancy projects, public speaking and training for a variety of public and private sector entities.

He is Chief Economist to the Friends First Group and was previously Treasury Economist at AIB (1987-1991) and Chief Economist at Bank of Ireland Group Treasury (1995-2000).

He is the author of the SIMI/DoneDeal Motor Industry Review and Friends First Quarterly Economic Outlook. He has a particular interest in tourism, regional development and the agri-food sector.

Jim writes a weekly column in The Examiner and is a frequent contributor to media. He also lectures on the MSc Management at Smurfit School of Business in UCD and is a frequent speaker at conferences and seminars both in Ireland and overseas.

He is a board member of Agri-Aware and Chairman of Love Irish Food. He is also Chairman of Three Rock Capital Management, an investment firm.

ALAN COX

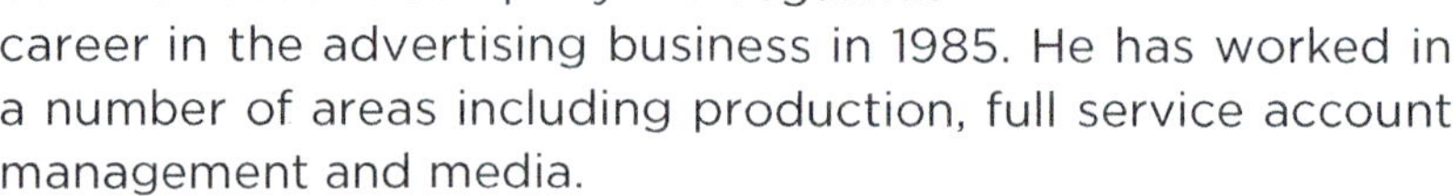

Alan Cox is Chief Executive of Core, Ireland's largest marketing communications company. He began his career in the advertising business in 1985. He has worked in a number of areas including production, full service account management and media.

Following four years as Media Director with Bell Advertising (part of Ogilvy & Mather), Alan was appointed Managing Director of Ogilvy's new media company, The Network, in 1997; he was appointed to the European Board of the company the following year. In 1999 he joined Carat Ireland where he spent seven years until his move to Core in September 2006.

In addition to his work in advertising, he spent a number of years working as a radio presenter in the 'pirate' days on stations including Radio Nova and Capitol Radio and retains a keen interest in the medium.

He has worked on various industry committees, including the Joint National Listenership and Outdoor Research bodies. He served a two-year term as Chairman of TAM Ireland, the company that manages the television viewing research contract from 2012 to 2014.

Core has been voted *Agency Network of the Year* for the last four years at the Irish Media Awards. The company was also voted one of the top three workplaces in Ireland by the *Great Place to Work Institute* for the last four years.

ACKNOWLEDGEMENTS

The authors would like to thank the following people for their assistance and guidance in relation to the content of this book.

Dr. Veli Bicer

Breda Brown

Trish Carey

Patrick Coveney

Jennifer Cruise

Barry Dooley

Craig Farrell

Peter Field

Aidan Greene

Maryam Hussain

Dr. Philip Lyons

Melanie O'Donovan

Eddie O'Mahony

Andy Pierce

FOREWORD

BARRY DOOLEY
CHIEF EXECUTIVE OFFICER
ASSOCIATION OF ADVERTISERS IN IRELAND

On behalf of the Association of Advertisers, I am delighted to welcome this comprehensive book, *Marketing Multiplied*.

This is the first ever study, of this scale, that reviews the impact of marketing communications from both a macroeconomic and microeconomic basis. The book surveys the global repository of economic literature to demonstrate the significant contribution that advertising makes to national economies. It also brings together many proof points that describe the effectiveness of marketing communications in driving growth for companies and brands.

One growing concern relates to the increase of short-term marketing. This shift has been caused by recession-driven urgency, which is damaging to the profitability of marketing. Now, more than ever, there is a requirement to ensure that the marketing ethos informs the boardroom agenda. It's time for marketers to regain control; marketing should be seen as the engine room and not as a service function.

Throughout this book you will see how advertising, in particular, has an important role to play in a market economy. A strong economy requires a vibrant marketing industry. The book is unequivocal on the fact that advertising and the economy are positively correlated and that increased advertising boosts growth, in a material way.

Marketing really matters. It's an economic catalyst, driving competition and innovation. It enriches the brands that people enjoy and trust. It contributes to society, not least by funding independent, varied media and fundamentally, it facilitates choice.

I would like to thank the authors, Chris Johns, Jim Power and Alan Cox. This book should be on the desk of anyone who is serious about improving the performance of marketing communications in their business.

EXECUTIVE SUMMARY

Economics has plenty of useful things to say about marketing and often takes a much more positive view of it than is commonly supposed.

Since the nineteenth century, economists have analysed and argued about advertising. But from both a theoretical and empirical perspective the position is clear: advertising is good for growth, promotes competition, helps innovation and leads to lower prices.

The point about growth is worth emphasising; it is the least studied link to advertising. The evidence strongly suggests that advertising is extremely important for the overall level of economic activity; it oils the wheels of economies, provides jobs and boosts growth in an unambiguously positive way. We argue that the evidence is clear about the influence of advertising on economic growth: it is positive and large. The debate is mostly about the size of that effect. Researchers have found, for example, that €1 of advertising generates €5.70 on average for the Irish economy.[1] Other research across different countries finds similar, often larger, effects.

[1] Deloitte. *Advertising: An Engine for Economic Growth*. October 2013.

Economists have paid much more attention to advertising's relationship with competition, innovation and prices. Again, the evidence points to robust conclusions: advertising promotes competition, boosts innovation and helps to lower prices. These effects are, in our view, at least as significant as the relationship between advertising and the macro economy.

Advertising is controversial, more so than its economic importance would justify; there has been a traditional distaste for it among intellectuals and economists. Over the years, economists have typically argued that it is wasteful, manipulative and anti-competitive. One economist even argued that the single redeeming feature of advertising was that it provided a source of revenue for the press. Our analysis discredits this blinkered and inaccurate view.

Advertising has an important role to play in a market economy. It provides consumers with information; it improves consumer choice and consumer welfare; it enables producers to increase sales, thereby boosting revenues, employment and overall economic activity; it enhances competition and can erode excess profits by increasing competitive forces.

The case studies outlined in this book represent a tiny portion of available evidence demonstrating the effectiveness of advertising and marketing campaigns. They cover a cross section of business types and geographic regions. All show the same results – namely, that advertising and marketing campaigns can have a significant influence on the growth and profitability of businesses.

The value of creativity in marketing communications is proven and quantifiable. Of all the factors that are within the marketer's sphere of influence, this is the most important by far. The choices made in relation to investment in creativity have a profound impact on the growth in profitability of brands. Creatively-awarded campaigns are six times more efficient than non-awarded campaigns in growing market share.[2]

[2] Field, Peter. *Selling Creativity Short*. UK: Institute of Practitioners in Advertising (IPA) and Thinkbox. 2016.

Recruiting new customers is more profitable than trying to increase frequency of purchase. Compelling evidence supports the contention that loyalty programmes have little effect and when they work, they do so by mainly recruiting new customers, not by reducing churn or by extracting more value from existing ones.[3]

The size of a brand has a major impact on the efficiency and effectiveness of marketing communications.[4 & 5] Large brands have inherent advantages over smaller brands; they have higher penetration, better distribution, stronger range and pricing strategies that help to maintain and increase share.

Short-term marketing is on the rise and it is damaging the profitability of marketing. Long-term campaigns are approximately three times more efficient than short-term campaigns. Short-term initiatives are more effective at driving transient sales effects, but they deliver weak long-term growth. Businesses need to employ both techniques, but in the correct proportion.[6]

Emotionally-based campaigns outperform rationally-based campaigns on every business measure; they are significantly more profitable, they are better at generating awareness, they are stronger at creating differentiation and they form more durable memories of brands in the minds of consumers.[7]

On average, marketers should spend 60% of their budget on brand-building activity (long-term, broad reach, emotional) and 40% on sales activation (short-term, tightly targeted and information rich), to achieve maximum efficiency and maximum effectiveness.[8]

3 Binet, Les and Field, Peter. *Marketing in the Era of Accountability*. UK: Institute of Practitioners in Advertising (IPA) and Warc. 2007.
4 Jones, John P. *Ad Spending: Maintaining Market Share*. Harvard Business Review, 68(1). 1990.
5 Nielsen and IPA. *How Share of Voice Wins Market Share*. UK: Institute of Practitioners in Advertising (IPA) and Nielsen Analytic Consulting. 2009.
6 Field, *Selling Creativity Short*, pg 11.
7 Binet and Field, *Marketing in the Era of Accountability*.
8 Ibid.

Brands using paid media normally grow three times faster than those that rely on owned and earned media alone. Owned media typically increase the effectiveness of a paid campaign by 13%, while adding earned media causes an increase of 26%.[9]

Advertising is extremely important for economic activity; it oils the wheels of economies, provides jobs and boosts growth in an unambiguously positive way

9 Binet, Les and Field, Peter. *Marketing in the Digital Age*. UK: Institute of Practitioners in Advertising (IPA). October 2016.

PREFACE

The objective of this book is to provide evidence of the effectiveness and efficiency of marketing communications in driving national economies and brands. Marketing communications is quite a broad term that captures all the messaging and media used to communicate with a desired market. It includes branding, packaging, advertising, direct marketing, public relations, owned media, earned media, printed materials, sales presentations, merchandising, sponsorships etc.

Due to the broad canvas described above, it is not possible to measure, with precision, each and every element of the marketing communications activities of a brand or business. This is due to the lack of availability of relevant data for some of the channels within marketing communications. However, this problem does not exist in the area of advertising: high quality data relating to advertising activities are readily available in most markets and their impact can be measured through econometric modelling.

> Advertising is the main method used to promote goods and services, with an estimated spend globally of $542 billion in 2016

In some cases, it is possible to quantify the impact of other factors (e.g., creativity, the use of emotion in messaging, brand size, the role of brand building) and, where available, we have included proof of their effect. However, in most cases it is advertising specifically that is measured. Therefore, the term 'advertising' is seen more often than the term 'marketing' throughout this book.

Advertising is the main method used to promote goods and services, with an estimated spend globally of $542 billion in 2016.[10] The key media for advertising include online channels, radio, television, newspapers, magazines, direct mail, cinema and out-of-home formats.

Figure 1 shows the breakdown of global advertising expenditure in 2016. Television is still the dominant medium with 35.6% share of spend. Mobile advertising is the key driver of growth, with spend increasing by an estimated 48% in 2016. This increase in mobile investment is coming at the expense of print media, television and 'traditional' online desktop display. Growth in the internet advertising market is due to the increasing use of mobile devices such as smartphones and tablets, as well as an improvement in ad-measurement techniques. The growth in online is also being driven by 'paid search' advertising (+17%), which will continue to grow as *hyper-local* and *voice recognition* techniques allow for more relevant search results.

FIGURE 1: GLOBAL ADVERTISING EXPENDITURE BY MEDIUM (2016)

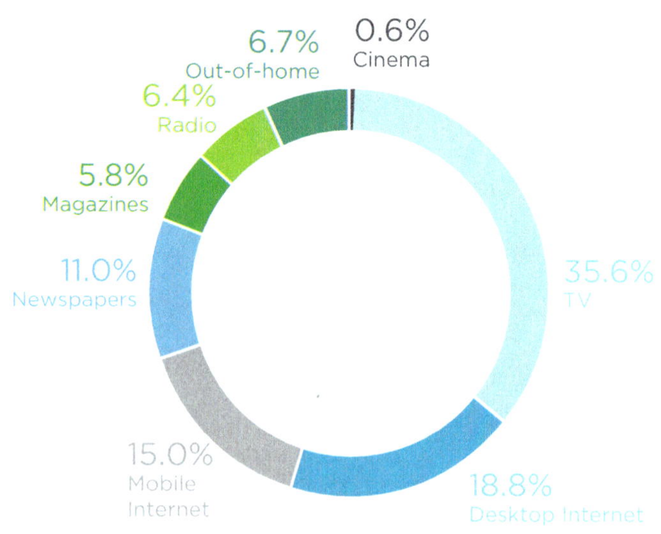

Note: Direct Mail is not measured

[10] Austin, Anne; Barnard, Johnathan; and Hutcheon, Nicola. *Zenith Advertising Expenditure Forecast*, December 2016.

Advertising has an important role to play in a market economy. It provides consumers with information; it improves consumer choice and, by implication, consumer welfare; it enables producers to increase sales, thereby boosting revenues, employment and overall economic activity; it enhances competition in the marketplace and can erode excess profits by increasing competitive forces.

In general, the main objective of marketing communications, in all of its forms, is to influence consumer perceptions and tastes in favour of a product or service. Marketing communications seek to increase consumer awareness of a product and, in the process, they consolidate the commitment of existing customers and attract new customers; the general intention is to shift the demand curve outwards to the right and gain market share. In other words, the objective of marketing communications is to increase demand for a good or service at any given price. This effect is caused by the positive impact that this messaging has on consumer behaviour.

We did not conduct any primary research for this book. Instead, our aim was to survey the compelling literature and research that already exists to present, in one location, a robust case for the extraordinary impact of marketing communications on national economies and brands. We also wanted to provide marketers with strong, evidence-based guidance on how to improve the effectiveness of their campaigns.

Marketing tends not to be taken as seriously by corporate boards as it should be. The reason for this has been the absence of quantified, credible evidence to demonstrate how essential marketing is to the long-term growth and profitability of businesses. We hope that this book plays a part in correcting this deficiency and persuades industry stakeholders to grow their knowledge base by prioritising investment in marketing analytics.

ECONOMICS, ECONOMISTS & ADVERTISING:
METHOD IN THEIR MADNESS?

There is an extensive literature - and accompanying debate and controversy - going back at least a century, on the economics of advertising. That literature, as is often the case in most areas of economics, is a combination of theory and evidence. It looks at the macro picture as well as the micro, the bottom up.

The above quotes illustrate the flavour of the debate contained within that literature: there is plenty of cynicism about economics, advertising and the way in which economists think about advertising. While understandable, much of that cynicism is misplaced. Economics has plenty of useful things to say about advertising and, as hinted at by the quote from Tim Duy, it often takes a much more positive view of advertising than is commonly supposed. Rory Sutherland, a well-known senior figure in the advertising industry - famous for his Ted Talks - puts the more familiar, negative, point of view regarding the lack of attention paid to advertising by economists.

[11] Taylor, Timothy. *The Case for and Against Advertising*. Conversable Economist. November 2012.

[12] Burke-Kennedy, Eoin. *Ad Man Sutherland Brings His Roadshow to Kilkenomics*. Irish Times. November 2015.

For all sorts of reasons, which we will explore more fully in this book, economists have been typically more concerned with micro aspects of advertising rather than the macroeconomic growth implications. A submission to a US congressional committee by two Nobel prize-winning economists (Kenneth J. Arrow and George Stigler) illustrates this point nicely:

'Advertising is a powerful tool of competition. It provides valuable information about products and services in an efficient and cost-effective manner. In this way, advertising helps the economy to function smoothly – it keeps prices low and facilitates the entry of new products and new firms into the market.'[13]

This is where economics has been focussed: on the 'efficiency' aspects of advertising rather than the impact on economic growth. The literature is rich in examples of how efficiency is improved in powerful ways. The growth literature is less extensive but also highly significant, in our view.

In part one of this book we look at the literature and associated methodological arguments. A very brief excursion into seemingly esoteric issues is important, because of the controversy and confusion that exist; and an understanding of what economics can contribute to the debate (a lot, in our view) requires a slightly deeper dive than is usual in studies such as this.

A small number of key themes weave their way through the work of most, if not all, economists who have looked at advertising. Those issues raised above by Arrow and Stigler, permeate the literature: what does advertising mean for growth, competition, innovation and consumer prices? These questions recur time and again, beginning with work done in the nineteenth century, to analysis conducted very recently.

[13] Stigler, George and Arrow, Kenneth J. *Miscellaneous Revenue Issues*. US: Government Printing Office. 1993.

The studies are, inevitably, of increasing sophistication but the answers, we believe, are consistent and clear: advertising is good for growth, promotes competition, helps innovation and leads to lower prices.

Here, we state our conclusions up front: first, at the macro level:

Advertising is extremely important for economic activity; it oils the wheels of economies, provides jobs and boosts growth in an unambiguously positive way. We argue that the evidence is clear about the influence of advertising on economic growth: it is positive and large. The debate is mostly about the size of that effect.

The return on investment from advertising - when done properly - is overwhelmingly positive

Second, at the micro level, looking at individual companies, the evidence is also clear:

The return on investment from advertising - when done properly - is overwhelmingly positive.

We believe that where there is debate, it is only about the size of these effects; the case for their existence is both intuitively obvious and present in many hard data points. The microeconomic impact of advertising is explored in detail in part two of this book.

PART 1:

THE MACROECONOMIC EFFECT OF ADVERTISING

CHAPTER 1

THE LITERATURE REVIEW

Kyle Bagwell (2005)[14] provides a useful and comprehensive survey of both top down and bottom up economics, as well as theory and evidence. He starts by pointing out that pre-twentieth century economists were mostly uninterested in advertising. This is easily understood in the context of the dominant theoretical paradigm of that era: *perfect competition*. This is not the place for a detailed exploration of the methodology of economics, but a few words are necessary; this is, after all, a survey of the economic literature. Limitations and controversies within economics contribute to confusion, not just with the economics of advertising. It is important to be aware of the issues, even where they remain unresolved.

The early assumption of *perfect competition* is a particular example of how economists do their thing. Models of economic behaviour always involve simplifying assumptions; this is the only way complicated questions can be made tractable. The *only* way a map can accurately represent its subject with 100% precision is to be in three dimensions and be of the same size as the area in question. Economists use models in the same way cartographers use maps; but the economists' maps, simply because of the technology and data available, are in many respects like those drawn by mapmakers before the age of satellites.

Perfect competition, where firms are so small and plentiful that they are all price takers, i.e., they cannot control the market price of their product (no monopolies or oligopolies), is clearly an unrealistic assumption. Industry structures rarely follow this simple paradigm in practice.

14 Bagwell, Kyle. *The Economic Analysis of Advertising*. US: Columbia University Department of Economics, Discussion Paper Series (01). August 2005.

A vast literature exists about whether or not the simplifying assumptions embodied in *perfect competition* make sense and whether or not the models themselves are useful outside the classroom. It is an unresolved, but hugely important, debate. Advertising does not fit easily into many models of the overall economy; that simplifying assumption about *perfect competition* is one reason. Another is that macro models of the economy historically focus on the aggregates around which the national accounts are built: consumption, investment, government spending, exports and imports. This explains, in part, the relatively small amount of literature that focuses on advertising and the economy at large.

> It is a matter of empirical fact, established beyond all reasonable doubt, that advertising and national economies are positively correlated to a large degree

In these kinds of models, advertising is essentially assumed away. This has contributed to a contemporary, as well as historic, lack of interest in advertising by macroeconomists. The tools and techniques available to the big picture analysts tend to dictate the kinds of questions that can be tackled, from both a theoretical and an empirical perspective. Also, advertising is not something easily incorporated into contemporary models of the overall economy.

These issues (and others) mean that most investigations in economics amount to something like a trial before a jury: we try to establish things 'beyond reasonable doubt'. Claims to 100% certainty nearly always need to be treated with caution, because our theories and our data are often not up to that particular task. However, strong inferences and conclusions are still possible. In the case of advertising, there is a dearth of 'big picture' studies, as most attention has been directed at company or sector-specific analysis.

Also of great significance for any investigation of advertising is the methodological debate over cause and effect. Two or more things can be correlated, but it is often fiendishly difficult to infer which way causation runs. This question has bedevilled empirical analysis for centuries. The quantum of advertising expenditure and the associated growth rate of GDP is a particular example of this extremely common question: which causes which?[15]

In our view, it is a matter of empirical fact, established beyond all reasonable doubt, that advertising and national economies are positively correlated to a large degree. However, the question is, does increased advertising cause an economy to grow or does increased economic activity prompt firms to advertise more? Or could causation actually run in both directions? These questions of causality permeate the macro literature, both theoretical and empirical. While there are techniques that provide a tentative way of unravelling the correlation/causation problem, they are not definitive or conclusive. In the case of the macroeconomics of advertising, most economists move on to easier questions – another reason why the literature is so thin. There are, of course, honourable exceptions that attempt to sort out this question of causation, which we will describe later.[16]

It is important to state up front that there are good theoretical and empirical reasons for believing that causation runs both ways: advertising is good for the economy and vice versa. A healthy advertising industry is a good marker of a healthy economy. Indeed, economists and statisticians are always on the lookout for indicators of current and future economic conditions; leading indicators play an important role in many forecasting models. Advertising expenditure is surely a prime candidate for predicting the current and, perhaps, future state of the economy. The controversy is more about the measurement of these effects rather than their existence. We should not lose sight of this very important conclusion, one that can get lost in the methodological and statistical fog.

15 A classic study of the genre, which suggested a two-way street, by Ashley, Richard; Granger, Clive W. J.; and Schmalensee, Richard. *Advertising and Aggregate Consumption: An Analysis of Causality*. Econometrica, 48(5). 1980.

16 A 2013 Deloitte study (discussed in greater detail in Chapter 1.8) represents a state-of-the-art attempt to sort out, statistically, the problems of two-way causation. Deloitte finds, after adjusting for the causation/correlation problem, that advertising drives a significant portion of economic growth.

1.1 IS BIG DATA THE SOLUTION?

We conclude this passage of our study with a hypothesis: a lot of the questions around advertising and the macroeconomy will be resolved when we get more and better data. As Professor Noah Smith put it recently:

'...economics is now a rogue branch of applied math. Developed without access to good data, it evolved different scientific values and conventions. But this is changing fast, as information technology and the computer revolution have furnished economists with mountains of data. As a result, empirical analysis is coming to dominate economics.'[17]

This, of course, is the hope that 'big data' will answer some of our burning questions, including those about advertising.

17 Smith, Noah. *Economics Has a Math Problem*. Bloomberg. September 2015.

We think it will, but only from the bottom up. Big data will, it seems to us, furnish us with many more case studies, from which we will eventually be able to proceed to broad generalisations. We suspect that those macro conclusions will be the same as today: advertising is very good for the economy.

It is worth noting that this section's focus on the macroeconomy should not deflect from the much more numerous micro studies (discussed later in this book) which provide a large body of evidence that clearly demonstrates the positive effects of advertising for individual brands.

A lot of the questions around advertising and the macroeconomy will be resolved when we get more and better data

---

BOX 1

A survey of surveys

This book is not the first survey of this topic. Indeed, in at least one respect, we present a kind of meta-study, a survey of surveys. We mention Bagwell (2005)[18] several times as an excellent example of the survey literature.

All researchers, whether in the private or public sector, try to impress with both quality and quantity. Understandably, it is common practice to try to convince the reader how hard we have worked. What is rarely acknowledged is that few people, outside academia at least, will ever have the time or inclination to access and read the copious references provided, each of which is often lengthy and dense. Bagwell, for example, runs to 181 pages, and that is just one paper. Short, easily digestible, surveys are notable for their rarity but one is to be found in the Concise Encyclopaedia of Economics[19] where Professor George Bittlingmayer provides one of those rare examples. Here, we survey his short survey.

Bittlingmayer dates the beginnings of the economic analysis of advertising to the 1930s and 1940s. He correctly notes that *'critics and defenders have often adopted extreme positions, attacking and defending any and all advertising'*. His survey is in the context of the US market, but it has general applicability. He observes that advertising, as a percentage of US GDP, has stayed roughly constant since the 1920s (2%). However, advertising intensity varies greatly across firms and industries (a pattern common in many countries).

18 Bagwell, *The Economic Analysis of Advertising*, pg 23.

19 Bittlingmayer, George. *Advertising*. The Concise Encyclopaedia of Economics: Library of Economics and Liberty. 2008.

Early critics of advertising focused on the possibility of entry barriers leading to monopoly. Bittlingmayer points us to research that shows the correlation between advertising intensity and monopoly power is low. In fact, research shows that advertising promotes competition rather than monopoly. Some researchers use profitability, in particular rates of return, to argue that advertising creates monopoly power.

However, Bittlingmayer refers us to research that properly measures invested capital; when advertising is treated as investment spending, those 'monopoly' rates of return tend to disappear. He directs us to research that shows how advertising promotes competition and lower prices.

Advertising promotes competition and lower prices

Finally, Bittlingmayer points us to the relative scarcity of research that looks at the many different ways advertising is deployed by governments to promote better behaviours, such as proper diet, less drinking, better driving etc.

We, on the other hand, have some specific examples of how advertising has been used as a powerful driver of social change in part two of this book.

1.2 BEGINNING TO ATTRACT ATTENTION

The relative lack of interest in advertising by economists in the nineteenth century wasn't just because their models assumed advertising didn't exist. As Bagwell points out, there wasn't that much actual advertising around (relatively speaking), at least not until the turn of that century. Bittlingmayer (see Box 1) suggests that modern advertising began in the early twentieth century with the advent of two new products, Kellogg's cereals and Camel cigarettes. He also claims that the first product endorsement occurred in 1905 when baseball legend Honus Wagner's autograph was imprinted on the *Louisville Slugger* bat.

But once advertising did enter mainstream business, it began to attract the attention of economists. Even so, the incorporation of advertising into conventional economic theory wasn't accomplished in a material way until 1933 with the publication of Edward Chamberlin's seminal *Theory of Monopolistic Competition*.[20]

[20] Chamberlin, Edward. *The Theory of Monopolistic Competition: A Re-orientation of the Theory of Value*. US: Harvard University Press. 1933.

Chamberlin essentially introduced the notions of *persuasive* and *informative* advertising and developed a theme that has become common throughout many aspects of the literature: *theory on its own cannot provide conclusive or definitive answers to many of the questions that we ask*. For example, Chamberlin's modelling was unable to shed full light on what impact advertising is likely to have on pricing, which is a critical issue. As we shall demonstrate, more recent research has been able to explore both the theoretical and empirical evidence that advertising can both help competition and lower prices.

In terms of theory, there is a reasonably straightforward way to demonstrate the optimal amount of advertising for an individual firm and the latest thinking on this is covered in detail in part two of this book. A classic paper on this issue was written in 1962 by Marc Nerlove and Kenneth J. Arrow, *Optimal Advertising Policy Under Dynamic Conditions*.[21]

[21] Arrow, Kenneth J. and Nerlove, Marc. *Optimal Advertising Policy Under Dynamic Conditions*. Economica, 29(114). 1962.

Nerlove and Arrow make the case that advertising expenditures '*are similar in many ways to investments in durable plant and equipment*'. This is an important point, which is perhaps obvious to economists, that needs to be emphasised in the context of this book. This point also supports an important aspect of the survey by Bittlingmayer, discussed in Box 1. The authors extend an earlier (classic) study, by Robert Dorfman and Peter O. Steiner (1954),[22] to establish a theoretical decision rule for firms to maximise revenues. They argue that their model produced similar results to the rules of thumb actually used by many organisations, whereby firms keep a constant ratio of sales to advertising.

More recent research warns against this approach: a 2016 study by Abas Mirzaei, David Gray, Chris Baumann and Lester W. Johnson[23] found that *'unhealthy brands'* tend to set their advertising budget as a constant percentage of sales. The report went on to say that such brands are vulnerable to market threats and competitors' strategies. The authors advise that poor-performing brands need to develop long-term advertising-spending strategies that *'gently and regularly'* increase investment relative to competitors. This view is supported by work from Les Binet and Peter Field in their 2007 study *Marketing in the Era of Accountability,*[24] which recommends *share of voice* as a key metric in budget setting. This area is explored in detail later in the book (see Chapter 7).

An unusual and very recent piece of research is to be found in a study by Laurent Cavenaile and Pau Roldan (2016),[25] in which a number of themes covered in this book are explored. In particular, the authors investigate the role that advertising can play as a form of research and development (as mentioned, this is not common in the literature) and how it interacts with more 'traditional' forms of capital investment in innovation.

22 Steiner, Peter O. and Dorfman, Robert. *Optimal Advertising and Optimal Quality*. American Economic Review, 44(5). 1954.

23 Mirzaei, Abas et al. *Assessing Ad-Spend Patterns to Predict Brand Health: A Model for Advertisers to Determine Future Advertising-Budgeting Strategies*. Journal of Advertising Research, 56(2). April 2016.

24 Binet and Field, *Marketing in the Era of Accountability*, pg 12.

25 Cavenaile, Laurent and Roldan, Pau. *Advertising, Innovation and Economic Growth*. 2016.

The research also considers (although this is not its prime focus) how all of this affects overall economic growth. One important conclusion is that *'Overall, the economy grows more rapidly as advertising becomes more and more efficient'.*

The economy grows more rapidly as advertising becomes more and more efficient

1.3 TOP DOWN OR BOTTOM UP? THEORY AND EVIDENCE

Many - if not most - academic studies (both theoretical and empirical) are essentially micro in nature: they study advertising in the context of an individual firm, product or industry. As mentioned earlier, there is relatively little analysis of advertising and how it impacts the macroeconomy.

One aspect of much of the empirical literature is the extent to which advertising is a barrier to entry and therefore, a contributor to oligopoly or monopoly profits (usually cast in terms of an investigation of profit margins greater than implied by competitive price-cost relationships).

In this context, the question of regulation often arises. The behaviour of 'large' firms is often the focus of these kinds of studies, often from a 'Galbraithian' perspective, which is one that essentially takes it as given that regulation is needed to prevent the negative consequences of oligopolistic/ monopolistic behaviours.

There is an extensive body of research, along with large and growing data sets, that examines advertising at the firm and/or the sector level. This is what we mean by bottom up. And the evidence base - as we shall discuss in greater detail later in this book - provides strong empirical support for the ideas drawn from the more academic/theoretical and/or macroeconomic literature.

> Advertising is a form of capital investment, rather than operating expense, that produces returns above the cost of capital

Advertising is a form of capital investment, rather than operating expense, that produces returns above the cost of capital. This is particularly salient in the environment that prevails today, where the cost of capital is, arguably, at an all-time low. For an excellent discussion, in a bottom up context, of advertising and capital budgeting, see Binet and Field, 2007.[26]

[26] Binet and Field, *Marketing in the Era of Accountability*, pg 12.

1.4 PERSUADING OR INFORMING: A FALSE DICHOTOMY?

Bagwell (2005)[27] and many other economists build on Chamberlin's original work and suggest a classification scheme for advertising that consists of three types.

First, there is *persuasive* advertising that '*primarily affects demand by changing tastes and creating brand loyalty*'.

Advertising can be both persuasive and informative

A second type of advertising focuses on *information*. If the purpose of advertising is to convey to consumers needed information, then the conclusions are usually quite different when compared to persuasive models: informative advertising can lead to lower prices and lower entry barriers, for example.

[27] Bagwell, *The Economic Analysis of Advertising*, pg 23.

Just because a convention - categorising advertising into these two different types - has been widely adopted doesn't necessarily make it right. It would seem reasonable to point out that advertising can be both persuasive and informative.

Later, in part two of this book, we discuss the role that emotion can play in the effectiveness of advertising and demonstrate that 'emotional' advertising is more likely to achieve better business results than 'rational' communications, which rely on information to persuade consumers (see Chapter 9).

The third type, *complementary* advertising takes a particular view of how advertising enters a typical consumer's *utility function*. In this class of model, it sometimes arises that the market provides too little advertising from the point of view of the consumer. The basic idea here is that consumers can be persuaded or informed about products and services they don't currently consume. In addition - or alternatively - their existing preferences can be reinforced: they might consume more of what they currently like and/or be informed about an alternative, but similar, product that enhances their existing experience. At its most basic, complementary advertising encourages consumers to switch brands.

Alternatively, it could be that these distinctions are arbitrary and, in fact, take a very negative view of how people form their tastes and spending decisions. Implicit in the *persuasive* view is the notion that we can, indeed, be persuaded. However, sometimes we are persuaded against our better nature. Box 2 explores these - perhaps philosophical - themes in greater detail.

We are inclined to think that there is a contradiction within the economics profession. On the one hand, much is made of rational, utility-maximising consumers. On the other, many economists seem to believe that people are persuaded to buy things they don't necessarily need. The two positions do not sit easily with each other.

BOX 2

Fools some or all of the time?

In *Phishing for Phools,*[28] George A. Akerlof and Robert Shiller (two Nobel prize winners) take aim at many aspects of modern economic life, not just advertising. They develop a critique of advertising that is, in our view, flawed. It is essentially based around two ideas.

First, advertising, in the language of our survey, is mostly (if not entirely) persuasive in nature. Secondly, and relatedly, the authors assert that most people fall for inappropriate advertising. We find neither of these notions persuasive, if we can be excused the pun. The title of the book says it all really. Rather than dwell on our own critique of the surprising (to us at least) ideas in the book, we draw attention to a review[29] by Alex Tabarrok, Professor of Economics at George Mason University.

[28] Akerlof, George A. and Shiller, Robert J. *Phishing for Phools: The Economics of Manipulation and Deception*. US: Princeton University Press. 2015.

[29] Tabarrok, Alex. *A Phool and His Money: Review of Phishing for Phools*. The New Rambler. 2015.

'The problem with these ideas is not that they do not contain a nugget of truth, but that the nugget doesn't lead to any obvious conclusion. Of course, producers in a modern capitalist economy sell us products that we don't really need. That's because capitalism has already taken care of our most basic needs. The richer society gets, the harder producers must work to sell.

Anyone can sell water in a desert but it takes real ingenuity to sell bottles of water to people who already have plenty to drink for free. Is bottled water stupid? Maybe so but then so is putting satellites into space so that every Rolling Stones song ever made can be played anywhere in the world from the palm of one's hand. Indeed, just about every good and service in modern society can be critiqued as unreal, unnecessary or unneeded.'

We could add plenty of other examples, but perhaps the most obvious is the Apple iPad: a product that many people initially criticised as 'unnecessary' has clearly enhanced lives and spurred further innovation. Steve Jobs famously said *'...it's really hard to design products by focus groups. A lot of times, people don't know what they want until you show it to them.'*[30]

The point, of course, is that it is a pretty arrogant perspective that calls consumers 'phools'; it resonates with our discussion of the deeper interpretation – and questioning – of persuasive advertising. Economics can't have it both ways: consumers can't be both 'rational utility-maximisers' and 'phools'.

[30] Burrows, Peter. *Back to the Future at Apple*. Bloomberg. May 1998.

1.5 IT ALL DEPENDS

The early theoretical models spawned a large empirical literature, particularly in the 1960s and 1970s, that concluded that different industries conform to different theoretical predictions: some advertising is persuasive, some is informative. General conclusions are noticeable by their absence. More recent work has allowed advances in game theory and behavioural models to extend the earlier, simpler, theoretical work.

Behavioural economics is a relatively new field - with few general macroeconomic predictions - that is being adapted to the analysis of advertising.[31 & 32] It was during this time, for example, that the complementary view first appeared. As before, these theoretical advances were followed up by a large empirical literature. We look at some case studies examining the effectiveness of advertising later in this book.

[31] Rory Sutherland, well known for his views on behavioural economics, approaches the 'persuasive' advertising question in characteristically blunt fashion: *'Whether you find out what people want, then devise a way to manufacture it or find out what you can manufacture and devise a way to make people want it - or a combination of both - you have created value just the same.'*

[32] Sutherland, Rory. *Branding Heterodox Economics*. Synthesis. November 2012.

The public policy implications of the literature are often industry-specific. While there are some general conclusions, the answer to the policy question is almost always 'it all depends'.

Broad or macro generalisations need to be treated with great care

Micro studies are almost always specific to the context in which they are set; broad or macro generalisations need to be treated with great care. It is worth stressing, however, that this is where the future of empirical research lies and we believe that it will reinforce positive views about advertising.

BOX 3

The bigger picture is not just about economic growth

Ferdinand Rauch, an Oxford University academic, identifies *'an old debate in economic theory'* (2012),[33] dating all the way back to Alfred Marshall (1919) about whether or not advertising raises or lowers consumer prices. This question is at the heart of many of the debates about advertising; any conclusion that suggests that advertising increases prices usually carries with it the direct policy implication that advertising should be taxed.

By contrast, if advertising is seen to lower prices, then one possible conclusion is that advertising should be encouraged, perhaps with favourable tax treatment or subsidies. The question about prices doesn't address any aspects of growth; if advertising lowers prices, it is a good thing, whether or not it boosts growth. But we would argue that if the conclusion is that prices are lower than they would otherwise be, there is a presumption that growth would be enhanced.

Rauch correctly points out that this is a variant on the *persuasive* versus *informative* question, the answer to which has important policy implications:

'...informative advertising might be welfare increasing [a technical term meaning that there are overall net benefits to the economy], and some models even suggest that a subsidy for informational advertising would increase welfare.'

[33] Rauch, Ferdinand. *Advertising and Consumer Prices*. VOX (CEPR Policy Portal). November 2012.

This is a policy suggestion flowing logically from the analysis – the tax system should encourage informational advertising.

The evidence suggests that the answer, when looking at specific products at least, is that some prices seem to rise, others fall.

In a 2011 study,[34] Rauch looked at an unusual *'natural experiment'*: Austria's introduction, in 2000, of a 5% tax on advertising (the only country in the OECD to do this, according to Rauch). Austria had imposed advertising taxes previously, but differing localities imposed varying rates. The new unified rate had the effect of raising and lowering taxes, depending on locality. This produced data that provided an answer to the question, 'what is the overall effect of an advertising tax on prices?'

Subsidies for informational advertising could be welfare enhancing

Crucially, Rauch showed that where the advertising was *informative* prices fell. Moreover, the economy-wide effect, in aggregate, was to reduce prices on average. This is consistent with the idea that most advertising is informative, and it suggests that a tax on advertising would be welfare reducing. It also suggests that subsidies for informational advertising could be welfare enhancing.

[34] Rauch, Ferdinand. *Advertising Expenditure and Consumer Prices*. UK: Centre for Economic Performance (CEP) Discussion Paper 1073. August 2011.

1.6 THE BIGGER PICTURE

Compared to the literature outlined above, there is a relative dearth of studies that investigate the links between advertising and the macroeconomy, the links between advertising and growth.

Jacques Bughin and Steven Spittaels of McKinsey, for example, in 2012[35] conducted (in their own words) a *'meta-analysis of numerous articles published in leading economic and marketing journals over the past 30 years, focusing on links between advertising and the performance of individual companies or economies as a whole. However, we found that most previous studies examined how GDP affects advertising spend, rather than the reverse.'*

We also conducted a similar analysis and came to similar conclusions.

[35] Spittaels, Steven and Bughin, Jacques. *Advertising as an Economic-Growth Engine.* McKinsey & Company. March 2012.

Robert Jacobson and Franco M. Nicosia (1981)[36] is an early (and rare) example of an attempt to look at advertising and the broader economy. These authors present a slightly different taxonomy of advertising.

Accordingly, there are several research traditions. The first looks at advertising of a specific brand, product or image. The second is the narrow empirical attempt to quantify advertising's contribution to sales of a specific product. The third investigates structure, conduct and performance of specific industries: this is where, for example, entry barriers and profitability are investigated. This is a very standard approach, common in textbooks.

It is a quantum jump to generalise the results of industry studies to the macro effects of advertising in an economy and society

[36] Nicosia, Franco M. and Jacobson, Robert. *Advertising and Public Policy: The Macroeconomic Effects of Advertising*. Journal of Marketing Research, 18(1). 1981.

As noted above, this is really where most of the existing literature is focussed. Jacobson and Nicosia argue that '*...the most clear-cut conceptual limitation of industry studies on the relationships between advertising and sales is that their findings cannot be generalised to the macroeconomic level....it is a quantum jump to generalise the results of industry studies to the macro effects of advertising in an economy and society'.*

We would echo this conclusion but with one caveat (a hypothesis really): the advent of 'big data' (see Chapter 1.1) could well provide enough evidence (lacking at the moment) via bottom up studies to provide definitive economy-wide conclusions.

Jacobson and Nicosia review the literature that looks at the macro question. The first study they discuss was published by N. H. Borden (1942).[37] This early research, which is inevitably primitive, found that advertising is essentially pro-cyclical (when the economy does well, so does advertising spend and vice versa). However, the magnitude of the effect is small. A small number of studies used similar techniques to reach broadly similar conclusions.

For advertising to be useful as a policy tool, there must be a causal relationship, not just a simple correlation, that runs from advertising to consumer spending rather than to GDP

Nothing, according to Jacobson and Nicosia, was learned about advertising and the wider economy until 1969. In that year, W. A. Verdon, C. R. McConnell and T. W. Roesler[38] asked whether advertising is a suitable tool for macroeconomic stabilisation policies: is advertising a proper instrument for macroeconomic policy, similar to government spending and taxation policies?

[37] Borden, Neil H. *The Economic Effects of Advertising*. US: Richard D. Irwin Inc. 1942.
[38] Verdon, W. A. et al. *Advertising Expenditures as an Economic Stabiliser 1945-1964*. Quarterly Review of Economics and Business, 8 (Summer). 1969.

To our knowledge, this was the first time this question appears in the journals and, indeed, is one of the very few times it has been asked. Sadly, this study was somewhat inconclusive: perhaps an unsurprising result, given what we have discussed thus far.

Vernon et al. looked at the correlation between advertising and macroeconomic variables (as did the other researchers mentioned). However, this is insufficient when thinking about policy implications: for advertising to be useful as a policy tool, there must, as we have mentioned several times, be a causal relationship, not just a simple correlation. Moreover, the causal relationship must run from advertising to consumer spending rather than to GDP and/or industrial production (which is how the research question had been traditionally framed until this point). But when the question was posed in this way, the results were still inconclusive (R. G. Ekelund and W. P. Gramm, 1969).[39]

Of the remaining half dozen or so studies reviewed by Jacobson and Nicosia, little by way of conclusive evidence emerged. The rest of their paper essentially consists of a proposal for a research agenda for future work in this area. Not many economists seem to have picked up on their suggestions. This is not because the question is uninteresting but, we would suggest, is because (a) the problem is so intractable, and (b) macroeconomics has struggled with departures from the *perfect competition* (many firms, none dominant in terms of pricing or other key behaviours) paradigm.

[39] Ekelund, Robert B. and Gramm, William P. *A Reconsideration of Advertising Expenditures, Aggregate Demand and Economic Stabilisation*. Quarterly Review of Economics and Business, 9 (Summer). 1969.

1.7 THE MODERN BIG PICTURE LITERATURE

Here we survey those modern macro studies that do exist. We look at the following, in no particular order of significance:

1. *Advertising Pays: How Advertising Contributes to the UK Economy.* (Advertising Association and Deloitte, 2013)

2. *Advertising Pays 2: How Advertising Can Unlock UK Growth Potential.* (Advertising Association and Deloitte, 2014)

3. *Advertising Pays: The Impact of Advertising on the Belgian Economy.* (Deloitte, Radd voor de Reclame/Conseil de la Publicité, 2015)

4. *Advertising Pays: The Economic Employment and Business Value of Advertising [Australia].* (Deloitte Access Economics, 2016)

5. *The Economic Impact of Advertising Expenditures in the United States.* (IHS Global Insight, 2010, 2014, 2015)

6. *Advertising: An Engine for Economic Growth [Ireland].* (Deloitte, 2013)

7. *Advertising and Economic Growth.* (PhD Thesis, Maximillien Nayaradou, 2006, published by the World Federation of Advertisers)

8. *Advertising as an Economic-Growth Engine.* (McKinsey & Company, 2012)

One obvious common denominator for these studies is the authorship of Deloitte. This well-known and highly respected consultancy has been commissioned by various bodies in numerous countries to research the economic impact of the advertising industry. Across all of these detailed pieces of (econometric) research there is a similarity of results: the association between GDP and advertising is large (that's the familiar correlation), is statistically significant (an important point for the more mathematically minded) and strong evidence of causation is produced. In other words, advertising helps to boost GDP.

In Belgium, for example, Deloitte [3] shows that €2.2 billion of advertising spend adds at least €13 billion to the economy. Similarly, in a recently published study of advertising and the Australian economy, Deloitte [4] finds that A$12.6 billion of advertising expenditures (almost 1% of GDP) brings benefits of A$40 billion to the overall economy. Deloitte makes the point that this is almost as big as the productivity value of the digital economy in Australia and larger that the accommodation and food services industry.

To a greater (mostly) or lesser extent, all of these studies see advertising as a significant contributor to growth, and in a meaningful, very precise, statistical sense, advertising causes economic growth.

This body of work has not received much wider attention. It would seem reasonable to suggest that while the direction of causality seems clear, the size of the effects looks large to most mainstream economists.

In a meaningful, very precise, statistical sense, advertising causes economic growth

For example, the 2015 update of the IHS study [5] finds that *'every dollar of ad spending supported, on average, about $19 of economic output (sales).'* Of course, this is not (quite) the same thing as arguing that the 'multiplier' for advertising expenditures is nineteen. If this was the claim, many, if not most, economists would suggest that the results strain credulity.

There is not much more to the literature on the casual links between advertising and economic growth. It is possible, in a wider review of the academic advertising literature, to draw attention to the positive aspects of advertising: informational efficiency, lower costs etc. However, other than to cite the eight studies listed above, it would be very hard to produce a publishable literature review that reached strong, robust conclusions about economic growth and advertising.

Those eight studies are high quality pieces of work; because they are not published in refereed academic journals they have yet, however, to enter the mainstream. Nevertheless, it seems to us that they are at least persuasive, if we can be pardoned for another pun.

It is also the case that what we have called the 'efficiency' aspects of advertising - competition, innovation and price-lowering - and the 'growth' consequences are not separable. Efficiency is highly likely to have a positive association with growth. Think about it this way: if 'all' advertising does is to improve the efficiency of an economy via a boost to competition, few economists would argue that the overall size of the economy would be left unaffected: lower inflation, more competition and increased innovation are all unambiguous positives in their own right but will, in all likelihood, have the happy by-product of more economic growth and a larger economy. It is merely a historical accident that economists have studied efficiency more than growth.

BOX 4
Multipliers

The 'multiplier' is an extremely controversial subject in economics. It is almost always discussed in the context of government spending (both current and capital expenditure): the fiscal multiplier. The question is always about whether or not a government can tame the business cycle – usually, can a government boost economic growth with extra spending? This is a subject that merits a separate book all of its own.

The recent global recession has reawakened interest in fiscal multipliers; interest had waned over recent decades as it is a subject that elicits strong views but little by way of conclusive evidence. The economics profession, over the period (roughly) 1975-2007 had settled into an (uneasy) consensus that either the government expenditure multiplier is negligible or, even if it is significant, monetary (interest rate) policy is a far more effective policy tool, both in theory and practice. Post-2007, interest reawakened in the size of the fiscal multiplier as interest rates fell towards zero in many countries. It has been argued, convincingly in our view, that the multiplier is at its highest when interest rates are constrained by *the zero lower bound* (when a central bank wants to reduce the interest rate, but can't because it is already at or near zero).

A good summary of modern thinking about the calculation of the size of the multiplier is to be found in Nicoletta Batini, Luc Eyraud and Anke Weber (2014).[40] Estimates of multipliers vary; however, nearly all such calculations suggest that the plausible range is zero to two. We mention the research on fiscal multipliers to put the studies of advertising and economic growth into context. If, as in the case of the Irish Deloitte report (see Chapter 1.8), the suggestion is that the multiplier is around six (compared to nineteen in the US, as suggested by the IHS study), it is unsurprising that this conclusion was challenging to policy makers.

[40] Batini, Nicoletta et al. *A Simple Method to Compute Fiscal Multipliers.* IMF Working Paper, 14/93. June 2014.

In 2012, AECOM conducted a study[41] where *'the advertising industry in Ireland can be estimated to have an overall economic multiplier of three'*. This number resulted from comparing €766 million of advertising's contribution to GDP, of which €255 million represents direct value added. So, the arithmetic is clear: 766/255 is roughly three. Here, the term 'multiplier' is being used quite correctly. However, recall the macroeconomist's focus on policy: he/she usually asks, if we increase public spending by 'X', what would be the accompanying rise in GDP?

That is what is more conventionally meant by the term 'multiplier'. It is not necessarily the case that if advertising spending was, say, doubled from €255 million to €510 million, that GDP would rise by €766 million. Other things would happen - some activity would be displaced or even disappear: that's what advertising, in part, achieves: competitive advantage.

Economists' focus on fiscal multipliers flows from a policy perspective: if we increased public spending, how much would GDP increase? Estimates of that number vary wildly but are rarely greater than a factor of two. Different economists occasionally use the word multiplier in different contexts, all equally correct, but answering different questions and/or making different points. So, the term 'multiplier' needs to be treated carefully.

However, the research underlying these studies is thorough and the econometrics sophisticated. Whereas the estimate of the size of the multiplier might be considered high, and the precise context always needs to be made clear, there should be less controversy over the direction and significance of the associated effects: increased advertising boosts growth, in a material way.

41 AECOM. *The Economic Impact of Advertising in Ireland.* Association of Advertisers in Ireland (AAI). May 2012.

1.8 THREE GLOBAL CONSULTANTS: DELOITTE, IHS AND MCKINSEY

DELOITTE

In January 2013, Deloitte Economic Consultants, in cooperation with the UK's advertising association, published the first of two significant studies of how much the industry contributes to the UK economy.[42 & 43] They found that £16 billion of advertising spend supported £100 billion of economic activity:

'We [Deloitte] estimate that advertising adds at least £100 billion to UK GDP by increasing the level of economic activity and increasing the productivity of the [UK] economy.'

The first report pointed out that a third of UK TV revenues comes from advertising, with jobs created in industries from photography to movies. Deloitte calculated that 550,000 people were in employment because of direct or indirect advertising revenues in the UK. But the effects of advertising were argued to be much broader than these headline numbers.

[42] Advertising Association and Deloitte. *Advertising Pays (UK)*, pg 48.
[43] Advertising Association and Deloitte. *Advertising Pays 2 (UK)*, pg 48.

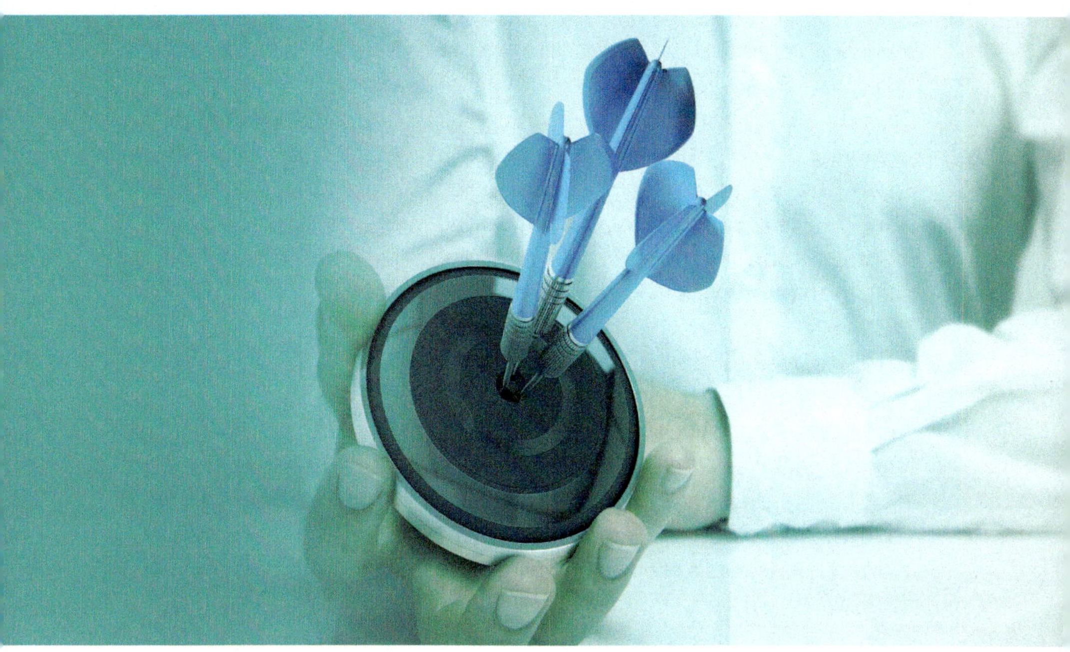

In particular, the roles that advertising plays in terms of stimulating competition, innovation and growth are critical. Deloitte makes an explicit reference to the same academic literature surveyed earlier in this book in arguing that increases in advertising expenditures boosts competition, improves product quality and helps to reduce consumer prices.

> Advertising adds at least £100 billion to UK GDP by increasing the level of economic activity and increasing the productivity of the UK economy

It is possible to interpret these results, derived from a rigorous statistical exercise, as simple 'multipliers': autonomous increases in advertising expenditure could lead to an increase in GDP along the lines suggested above.

A more nuanced interpretation of these numbers, bearing in mind our discussion of estimates of economic multipliers in Box 4, is that causation (which is at the heart of any multiplier analysis) is running both ways; increases in advertising spending do lead to significant overall economic effects, but the Deloitte numbers could also be picking up increases in economic activity (derived, say, from increases in technology or other types of capital investment) that boost advertising.

The statistical exercise conducted by Deloitte does try to control for these kinds of phenomena: they use advanced statistical techniques to deal precisely with this question. But we should nevertheless be careful before assuming that the size of the one-way causality running from advertising to GDP is as large as could be implied from the raw numbers. We are, nonetheless, on safe methodological grounds in arguing that the effect is both positive and large.

The follow-up 2014 UK report asked a different question, perhaps of a more micro nature. Critically, it found that smaller UK companies *'are significantly underweight in their use of advertising...and [the report] explains why that is stopping a sector full of talent and innovation from maximising its potential to create revenues, jobs and growth'.*

The report suggested that if only UK SMEs could raise their export performance to the EU average, £40 billion could be added to the UK economy. Clearly, advertising (and marketing) could aid in that goal. Deloitte's analysis suggested that *'an additional £1 on advertising would benefit an SME nearly eight times as much relative to its size as an equivalent £1 spent by a larger business'.* UK SMEs account for 18% of UK advertising spend but nearly 40% of turnover. A natural set of policy recommendations included giving help to SMEs with the short-term costs of advertising as well as more and better advice and support.

These two reports reflect, in part at least, the climate at the time. In 2013, attention was very much on the broader economy which was yet to show clear signs of full recovery from the preceding financial crisis. The question was asked: what can advertising do for growth? A year later, with GDP growth more assured, attention focussed on smaller companies. In a very clear sense, the two reports complemented each other.

€1 of advertising spend generates €5.70 on average for the Irish economy

Towards the end of 2013, the original Deloitte report was replicated for the Irish experience.[44] It was found that €1 of advertising spend generates €5.70 on average for the Irish economy. We would, again, draw attention to our comments on the statistical and other issues around the calculation and interpretation of multipliers, but we are again able to repeat our main substantive conclusion: the effect of advertising expenditure on the Irish economy is large.

As with the UK report, extensive analysis of the employment creation effects of advertising and the role it plays in competition and innovation all pointed to substantial positive effects for the Irish economy.

[44] Deloitte, *Advertising: An Engine for Economic Growth*, pg 10.

IHS GLOBAL INSIGHT

Like Deloitte, IHS has produced a number of reports on advertising and the economy, but with a focus on the US. In a 2015[45] study (building on earlier 2010[46] and 2014[47] analysis), IHS looked at seventeen industries, as well as the US government. The aim was to look at the effects of advertising across five economic 'dimensions'.

First, they considered the 'direct economic impact'. This focused on spending and jobs (over half a million people work directly in the US advertising industry) created in both the advertising industry and the sales and jobs created in the industries that were doing the advertising. Second, they looked at the impact (indirect) on sales and jobs *'supported by first-level suppliers to those industries that use advertising'*. Third, they went beyond those second-level suppliers to investigate all other sales and jobs effects. Finally, they considered the boost to consumer spending from all of the first three effects.

The results were striking: *'Every dollar of ad spending supported, on average, about $19 of economic output [and] for every million dollars spent on advertising, sixty-seven American jobs were supported across a broad range of industries.'* In 2014, that meant support for twenty million jobs, or 14% of total employment.

Some orthodox economists might, we suspect, recoil from the suggestion that the multiplier for advertising expenditures on the level of GDP is nineteen. Indeed, that might not, strictly, be what the IHS authors are arguing: 'support' is not quite the same thing as 'cause'. To provide some context, if not a lower bound for the advertising multiplier on GDP growth, Albert and Reid[48] suggested in 2011 that the number in the UK is two (although they also seem to think that a proper - full and final - accounting for third order effects means the multiplier is probably higher than this).

[45] IHS (Economics and Country Risk). *Economic Impact of Advertising in the United States*. The Advertising Coalition. March 2015.
[46] IHS (Global Insight). *The Economic Impact of Advertising Expenditures in the Unites States*. The Advertising Coalition. August 2010.
[47] IHS (Global Insight). *The Economic Impact of Advertising Expenditures in the United States, 2012-2017*. The Advertising Coalition. January 2014.
[48] Albert, Alexandra and Reid, Benjamin. *The Contribution of the Advertising Industry to the UK Economy*. Creative Industries and Credos. November 2011.

It is worth noting that a multiplier of two is much more in line with the analysis of fiscal multipliers discussed in Box 4; needless to say, it is an area fraught with methodological and empirical controversies and uncertainties. Even the word 'multiplier' can mean different things to different people and whatever its quantum, it varies according to the circumstances in question.

In any event, this kind of questioning should not deflect us from the main thrust of the analysis: the IHS findings for the United States economy are at one with those of Deloitte for the UK and Ireland: advertising spend has a large and positive effect on the economy.

It is worth spending a moment on the sheer scale of the US advertising industry: IHS reckons that by 2019, advertising expenditures will amount to $349.2 billion. In fact, according to Zenith the US accounted for a third of all advertising dollars spent around the world in 2016.[49]

IHS estimates that in 2014, $2.4 trillion (roughly 6.5% of the total) of direct sales were stimulated by advertising in the United States. Once the indirect effects are counted, the total amount of sales generated in the US economy, stimulated by advertising, amounted to $5.8 trillion, some 16% of the total.

Like Deloitte, IHS references the theoretical literature that we have surveyed above. Hence, we can clearly discern a common thread through over one hundred years of theoretical and empirical analysis.

IHS sums it up nicely: *'The benefits to the economy [are] a cost effective and timely mechanism for distribution of information about low prices and beneficial changes in technology and product design…it encourages lower prices…it speeds the implementation of new technology…it may encourage economies of scale.'*

[49] Austin et al., *Zenith Advertising Expenditure Forecast*, pg 16.

Those common threads are both big picture (more GDP growth) and micro (competition, efficiency, technological change and lower prices). We have noted these themes wherever we have looked in the literature. The only debate, in our view, is over their scale, not their existence.

> The total amount of sales generated in the US economy, stimulated by advertising, amounted to $5.8 trillion in 2014

MCKINSEY & COMPANY

The third leading global consultancy to have looked at the macroeconomic effects of advertising is McKinsey & Company (2012).[50] The arguments developed by McKinsey should by now be familiar: competition, information and pricing effects are discussed. As with the other two consultancies, McKinsey was interested in the impact on GDP growth (McKinsey also provides a detailed analysis of where in the US economy these effects are to be observed).

Again, the estimated size of the relationship is large: *'advertising has fuelled, on average, about 15% of growth for the major G20 economies over the past decade - and in some years, the contribution was as high as 20%.'*

It is worth noting that McKinsey addresses the statistical uncertainties of its work by stating that there is a less than 10% chance that they are wrong (in that advertising spending does not have a multiplier effect greater than one). This is how statisticians express, or quantify, how much uncertainty is around their results: they could be wrong, the multiplier could be a lot lower than their results suggest, but there is only a 10% chance of this. The precise statistical nature of this result gives a clue as to its antecedents - it builds on the earlier work, at least in part, referred to in our broad survey earlier, especially with regard to causality.[51]

Advertising has fuelled, on average, about 15% of growth for the major G20 economies

[50] Spittaels and Bughin, *Advertising as an Economic-Growth Engine*, pg 44.
[51] Ashley et al., *Advertising and Aggregate Consumption*, pg 25.

OTHER STUDIES

Maximilien Nayardou (2006)[52] begins by suggesting, not unreasonably in our view, that *'very little is known'* about advertising's impact on the wider economy. His approach is both original and echoes that taken by others in our survey: he looks at the relationship between consumption and advertising and how growth is enhanced via the concentration of advertising in fast growing sectors.

Advertising and innovation are highly correlated; competition is highest when advertising is also strong; advertising acts as a multiplier for economic growth.

Nayaradou is careful (rightly in our view) to emphasise correlation, rather than causation. He notes the positive correlation between advertising and economic growth; and he notes that countries with low advertising intensity also have tendencies to low relative economic growth. Nayaradou establishes links between advertising and economic efficiency – a common theme in our wider literature review. He provides another useful survey of the literature, echoing the points we have made in our own survey.

> To promote growth, the public authorities should encourage advertising investment in all of its forms, as this improves the productive efficiency of an economy

[52] Nayaradou, Maximilien. *Advertising and Economic Growth*. World Federation of Advertisers. 2006.

Nayaradou's detailed statistical analysis concludes:

'Whether for its impact on consumption, competition and the spread of innovation or for the stimulating effect of the growth of the advertising sector on average GDP growth, advertising investment has a positive impact on the economy.

The in-depth analysis of the statistics and data currently available generally comes out in support of the views of pro-advertising economists.... In order to promote growth, the public authorities should therefore encourage advertising investment in all of its forms, as this improves the productive efficiency of an economy.'

CHAPTER 2

BRINGING THE THREADS TOGETHER

Our objective for this part of the book is to provide the reader with a consensus view of the impact of advertising on the macroeconomy. We have surveyed all the significant literature around the world on this topic and the evidence is clear regarding the influence of advertising on economic growth: it is positive and large. Advertising is extremely important for economic activity; it provides jobs, promotes competition, helps innovation, leads to lower prices and boosts growth in an unambiguously positive way.

Advertising is certainly a controversial subject and over the years economists have often argued that it is wasteful, manipulative and anti-competitive. Our analysis discredits this inaccurate view, which is based on a disregard for the facts. It is a matter of empirical fact, established beyond all reasonable doubt, that advertising and national economies are positively correlated to a large degree.

Where things become less clear is about the size of the effect. There are a number of reports from global consultancy firms that put 'definitive' numbers on this. For example, Deloitte found that €1 of advertising spend generates €5.70 on average for the Irish economy[53] and McKinsey reported that advertising fuelled about 15% of growth for the major G20 economies.[54]

However, as we have said in this book, claims to 100% certainty nearly always need to be treated with caution, because the theory and data are often not up to that particular task.

[53] Deloitte, *Advertising: An Engine for Economic Growth*, pg 10.
[54] Spittaels and Bughin, *Advertising as an Economic-Growth Engine*, pg 44.

The big issue that continues to dog the research is causation: does advertising cause an economy to grow or does increased economic activity prompt firms to advertise more? Or could causation actually run in both directions? In our view, there are good theoretical and empirical reasons for believing that causation does run both ways: advertising is good for the economy and vice versa.

Then we come to the controversial subject of the 'multiplier'.[55] We must use this term carefully. The economist's definition of a fiscal multiplier stems from the question: if advertising spending is increased, how much would GDP increase? From an economist's perspective, the plausible range would be between one and two. In other words, for every €1 of investment, GDP could increase by up to €2. That is why the higher 'multipliers' quoted in the advertising-related macroeconomic research are questioned by economists. Also, the lack of clear evidence in the research that causation has been successfully factored in compounds the problem.

It is important to note that there is no debate regarding the multipliers reported in the microeconomic world of individual brands, where causation can be clearly proven. Here, it is quite credible for brands to expect profit to grow by a multiple of five or higher, as reported in part two of this book. However, the enormously complex subject of macroeconomics is substantially more challenging to unpick.

The purpose of advertising is to achieve growth and almost every euro invested in it is focused on that goal. This cannot be said of most other areas of economic investment. Advertising is a key engine of the economy and it should be stimulated by government policy rather than neglected or taxed.[56]

We urge the industry to continue to invest in research that sheds more light on this neglected area of economics. Many of the questions raised in this book will be resolved when we get more and better data. Advancements in data science and technology will also help. The advent of 'big data' could well provide enough evidence (lacking at the moment) via bottom up studies to provide definitive economy-wide conclusions.

[55] Batini et al., *A Simple Method to Compute Fiscal Multipliers*, pg 52.
[56] Rauch, *Advertising Expenditure and Consumer Prices*, pg 43.

PART 2:
THE MICROECONOMIC EFFECT OF MARKETING COMMUNICATIONS

CHAPTER 3

CONVINCING THE BOARDROOM

In part one of this book, we focused on the macroeconomic impact of advertising, and we outlined many examples of its significant and positive economic impact. We are now turning to the role that marketing communications play at a microeconomic level, for individual businesses and brands. Here, the picture becomes sharper. The analysis is less complex; there are fewer variables and data science is up to the task.

There are hundreds of case studies available that prove and quantify the extensive contribution that marketing makes to businesses every day. It is a true growth engine. This part of the book provides a summary of some of the most compelling case studies in existence. There are many more examples that can be found in archives throughout the world including the Warc Archive,[57] the Cannes Lions Archive,[58] the Effie Worldwide Library,[59] the Account Planning Group Archive,[60] the IPA Effectiveness Hub[61] and the IAPI ADFX Databank,[62] among others.

We would like to call out, in particular, the work carried out Les Binet and Peter Field for the *Institute of Practitioners in Advertising* (IPA) in the UK, beginning with the study *Marketing in the Era of Accountability*,[63] published in 2007, which analysed 880 case studies from the IPA Effectiveness Databank to identify the marketing practices and metrics that increase profitability. This landmark study was followed in 2013 by *The Long and the Short of It*,[64] which focused on the tension between short-term response activity and long-term brand-building.

57 Warc. (See www.warc.com for more).
58 Cannes Lions Archive. (See www.canneslionsarchive.com for more).
59 Effie Worldwide. (See www.effie.org for more).
60 Account Planning Group. (See www.apg.org.uk for more).
61 IPA Effectiveness Hub. (See www.ipa.co.uk/effectiveness/case-studies for more).
62 IAPI ADFX Databank. (See www.adfx.ie/databank for more).
63 Binet and Field, *Marketing in the Era of Accountability*, pg 12.
64 Binet, Les and Field, Peter. *The Long and the Short of it: Balancing Short and Long-Term Marketing Strategies*. UK: Institute of Practitioners in Advertising (IPA). 2013.

The next phase of their work was unveiled in October 2016, with the first instalment of a report entitled *Marketing in the Digital Age*[65] - a study into marketing best practice at a time of mature, experienced usage of digital media. The IPA is to be commended for its vision and consistent investment in bringing further knowledge to this sector.

Parallel to this, Field has been researching the role that creativity plays in campaign effectiveness for Thinkbox and the IPA. His first study, *The Link Between Creativity and Effectiveness (2010)*,[66] proved that advertising campaigns with high levels of creativity are far more efficient at increasing market share. Field continued to build on this work with the publication in 2016 of *Selling Creativity Short*.[67]

In addition to providing an update on his previous study, the report revealed evidence of the dramatic shift to short-termism in marketing and how it is damaging the effectiveness of creativity and the return on investment it generates.

These studies are absolutely essential reads for anyone working in the business. The findings of Binet and Field's work are referred to throughout this book.

> 80% of CEOs in Europe, USA, Asia and Australia believe that marketers are 'disconnected from business results'

Historical evidence is essential to the marketing industry; it helps to build credible cases for investment and it provides clear learnings in relation to the building blocks of effective strategies.

65 Binet and Field, *Marketing in the Digital Age*, pg 13.
66 Field, Peter. *The Link Between Creativity and Effectiveness*. UK: Institute of Practitioners in Advertising (IPA). 2010.
67 Field, *Selling Creativity Short*, pg 11.

John Fanning, a highly-respected practitioner in Ireland, put it well in his 2015 study *I Must be Talking to My Friends*:

'We are a business that is obsessed with change, which sometimes leads to a neglect of the accumulated experience and wisdom that has been built up over the years. We have built up an impressive corpus of knowledge about how marketing communications work. The IAPI ADFX case studies are an important contribution to that knowledge and the more we can quote them in support of presentations for investing in marketing communications, the more likely we are to be successful.' [68]

But there is a problem: boardrooms have not yet been convinced and claims made by marketing professionals are treated with some scepticism by senior management. In fact, marketing is among the least understood drivers of corporate performance.

Karen Hand and Jill McGrath wrote an excellent report on marketing effectiveness in 2015, *A Line in the Sand.*[69] In the introduction, they refer to the lack of respect for marketing in boardrooms; they quote a study from 2012 that found that 80% of CEOs in Europe, USA, Asia and Australia believe that marketers are *'disconnected from business results'*, 78% believed that marketing *'focuses on the wrong areas'* and 65% believed that marketing is stuck in *'marketing la-la land'.*

Given this perception, it is not surprising that marketers are severely under-represented on the boards of large companies. An article in Forbes in January 2016[70] brought the issue into sharp focus. In a study of the S&P 1500 (an index of top US companies), only 2.6% of 65,000 board members had managerial-level marketing experience - an astonishing statistic. In the UK, only 21% of FTSE 100 CEOs had a marketing background in 2015.[71]

[68] Fanning, John. *I Must Be Talking to My Friends*. Institute of Advertising Practitioners in Ireland (IAPI) and Television Audience Measurement Ireland (TAM Ireland). 2015.
[69] Hand, Karen and McGrath, Jill. *A Line in the Sand*. Institute of Advertising Practitioners in Ireland (IAPI) and Television Audience Measurement Ireland (TAM Ireland). 2015.
[70] Whitler, Kimberly A. *Why Few Marketers are Invited to Join Boards of Directors*. Forbes. January 2016.
[71] Econsultancy and Oracle Marketing Cloud. *Marketers in the Boardroom*. November 2015.

Certainly, boards can be criticised for being so uniformed as to devalue the role of marketing, but, in our view, the responsibility for this situation rests with the marketing communications industry. The industry has not invested sufficiently in proving its case. This may have been excusable in the distant past, when measurement techniques were more intuitive and less reliable, but that is no longer the case.

Patrick Coveney, CEO of Greencore Group plc and Chairman of Core put it well:

'The absence of marketers from boards cannot be good for companies; it means that a critical part of the business is not being given sufficient voice or respect and it goes a long way to explain why marketing budgets are thought of as an expense rather than an investment. Boards tend to be dominated by people with financial or engineering backgrounds, who are not necessarily trained to understand the consumer, the competitor landscape and external environment in a way that a skilled marketer can.

Boards often explain this shortcoming by saying that marketing is a tactical rather than a strategic pursuit and therefore has less of a place in the boardroom. This is plainly ridiculous. Of course, this challenge cuts both ways - marketers need to 'up their game', to make their input, agenda and style more relevant to their board peers. What's needed here is to configure senior management teams and corporate boards with complementary skills; to embrace diversity of thought; to balance creativity, analytics and performance discipline.'[72]

The role and practice of marketing is changing and the ultimate destination is to get to a stage where marketing insights, and creative ideas, are devised using data analytics as a core ingredient in the decision-making process. The advances in data science will bring us to a point where marketers will be able to predict outcomes for brands based on thousands of case studies and billions of data records.

72 Coveney, Patrick. *The Advertising Evangelist*. Business & Finance CEO 100 edition. October 2016.

In such a hyper-digitised age, when brand identity is vulnerable and loyalty can't be taken for granted, it is essential that we recognise the value of marketing and place it at the centre of our businesses. While embracing the opportunities that technology and data analytics now offer, let's not forget the importance of creativity and innovation to business performance.

It is essential that we recognise the value of marketing and place it at the centre of our businesses

CHAPTER 4

TYPICAL RETURN ON MARKETING INVESTMENT (ROMI) LEVELS

In its *Advertising Pays 2* report, which was published by the UK Advertising Association in 2014,[73] Deloitte used econometric modelling to estimate the absolute and marginal impact of changes in advertising investment levels on turnover, depending on the size of companies.

Unfortunately, as this study was conducted on a market-wide basis, it isn't possible to show the absolute return on marketing investment in terms of net profit. The closest we can come to measuring return on investment is to look at sales revenue, in this case.

The Deloitte study found that for every £1 invested in advertising, sales increased by £6, on average, across all firm sizes. However, it established that the absolute impact of advertising is greater for larger firms. By comparing the sample for subsets of small and large companies, Deloitte's econometricians found that the average impact of advertising on sales was an increase of £10 (for every £1 invested) for large firms and £2 for SMEs.[74] This is an indication that larger companies are more effective in transforming advertising investment into turnover because of their size.

73 Advertising Association and Deloitte. *Advertising Pays 2 (UK)*, pg 48.
74 Ibid.

However, the report goes on to say that advertising increases turnover at a greater speed in smaller companies. As mentioned earlier in this book, Deloitte estimated that an additional £1 invested in advertising by an SME has eight times the effect on sales relative to its size, compared to the impact of an extra £1 for a large business.[75]

The findings from this Deloitte report compare favourably with analysis conducted by the data scientists at Core. The team carried out meta-analysis of thirteen econometric studies conducted for Core clients between 2014 and 2016. The advertisers examined in the meta-analysis span eight industries including insurance, banking, automotive, fast-moving consumer goods, retail, transportation, utilities and entertainment.

The analysis found that €1 invested in advertising typically delivers a **revenue return** on marketing investment of €8.26 and a **net return** on investment of €5.44 for brands operating in Ireland.[76]

[75] Advertising Association and Deloitte, *Advertising Pays 2 (UK)*, pg 48.
[76] Core, *Core Meta-Analysis*, 2016.

€1 invested in advertising typically delivers a revenue return of €8.26 and a net return of €5.44 for brands operating in Ireland

CHAPTER 5

THE PROBLEM WITH RETURN ON INVESTMENT

In their studies into marketing effectiveness, Binet and Field consistently call out the danger of focusing exclusively on *return on marketing investment* (ROMI) as the principal *key performance indicator* (KPI). ROMI is important, but it must be remembered that it is a measure of **efficiency** and not necessarily **effectiveness**. They defined the differences between these KPIs in their report, *The Long and the Short of It*,[77] as follows:

*'**Efficiency** is essentially a measure of what is achieved per unit of investment made. This is where ROMI comes in. It enables us to look at how hard a group of campaigns worked, not merely what they achieved.'*

*'**Effectiveness** essentially means scale of effect – usually measured in terms of profit or market share growth. These are simple measures of what is achieved and do not relate the effect to the level of investment made to drive the effect.'*

[77] Binet and Field, *The Long and the Short of It*, pg 69.

If a marketer is obsessed with increasing return on investment exclusively, it can lead to strategies that are too narrow

Although there is often a correlation between effectiveness and efficiency, this is not always the case. If a marketer is obsessed with increasing ROMI exclusively, it can lead to strategies that are too narrow, both in terms of the audiences they target and the media they use.

Ultimately, it is the effectiveness of marketing in terms of absolute payback (i.e., growing brands and profit) that matters most. Field commented on this at *Effectiveness Week*[78] in London in October 2016:

'Return on investment is very dangerous if it's used in isolation or used as a dominant metric. It's an efficiency metric that will always flatter and reward sales activation strategies that are simply targeting customers in the market now and are doing nothing to build long-term growth. These activities tend to generate the most impressive ROIs, because it is easier to do; you get big spikes for relatively little investment because you target tightly.'[79]

Binet added: *'ROMI is not the thing that we should be focusing on. You can increase ROMI and make less money. That's the paradox and some people can't get their heads around it.'*[80]

To illustrate the issue, Binet and Field shared the results of correlation analysis that they had conducted to identify the top drivers of profit. They found that the most important individual metrics for profit were sales gain (40% correlation with profit), market share (23%) and penetration (21%). Return on marketing investment, on the other hand, had a correlation of just 15% with profit.[81]

78 Binet and Field, *Marketing in the Digital Age*, pg 13.
79 Ibid.
80 Ibid.
81 Ibid.

In their paper from 2004, *Measuring Marketing Productivity: Current Knowledge and Future Directions*, Roland Rust et al.[82] wrote, '*Maximisation of ROI as a management tool is not recommended (unless management's goal is efficiency rather than effectiveness), because it is inconsistent with profit maximisation - a point that has long been noted in the marketing literature (e.g., Robert S. Kaplan and Allan D. Shocker 1971* [83]*).*'

> You can increase return on investment and make less money - that's the paradox and some people can't get their heads around it

The other problem with ROMI is that it is an ambiguous metric that is often misinterpreted and miscalculated. It is important that we understand exactly what it means and how to measure it. This was the subject of a paper by four US marketing science and academic leaders published in the peer-reviewed journal, *Applied Marketing Analytics*.[84] They set out to clarify both the concept of ROMI and how companies should go about measuring and applying it. Paul Farris of the University of Virginia Darden School of Business, Dominique Hanssens of UCLA Anderson School of Management, James Lenskold of Lenskold Group and David Reibstein of The Wharton School joined forces on the project. Their definition is:

'ROMI is the financial value (net profit) attributable to a specific set of marketing initiatives (net of marketing spend), divided by the marketing cost 'invested' or risked for that set of initiatives.'

82 Rust, R. T., et al. *Measuring Marketing Productivity: Current Knowledge and Future Direction.* Journal of Marketing, 68(4). 2004.

83 Kaplan, Robert S. and Shocker, Allan D. *Discount Effects on Media Plans.* Journal of Advertising Research, 11(3). 1971.

84 Farris, Paul, et al. *Marketing Return on Investment: Seeking Clarity for Concept and Measurement.* Applied Marketing Analytics, 1(3). 2015.

Here is the formula:

$$\text{ROMI} = \frac{\text{Incremental financial value (net profit) generated by marketing minus the cost of marketing}}{\text{Cost of marketing}}$$

The key point to note here is that ROMI relates to the **incremental profit** generated by the marketing activity. However, it is often the case that practitioners insert incremental sales revenue in the above formula instead, which grossly exaggerates the true financial payback to the business. Additional revenue is not equal to additional profit; the extra costs associated with the incremental sales must also be considered.

Sometimes, when profit margins are unknown or undisclosed, it is acceptable to use revenue (in place of profit) as a guide, but in such circumstances, it should be clearly flagged as 'Revenue ROMI'.

Elsewhere in this book, we write about the relationship between short-term and long-term marketing (see Chapter 8). Marketing initiatives that are geared to short-term results do well in terms of payback (in the short run), but are significantly outperformed by longer-term brand-building campaigns. This poses problems for the calculation of marketing payback.

Therefore, a different approach is required when marketers want to assess the likely payback of future endeavours. Binet and Field favour *discounted cash flow analysis* (DCF);[85] accountants use this method for calculating the payback from longer-term investments. Because money in the future is worth less than money now, estimates of costs and revenue are discounted at a suitable interest rate. The resultant number is called the *net present value* (NPV) of the project. If this number is negative, the strategy being evaluated should be rejected; if it is positive, it should be approved.

[85] Binet and Field, *Marketing in the Era of Accountability*, pg 12.

We agree that the DCF approach is a worthwhile way of forecasting and evaluating different marketing strategies and that it is superior to ROMI in that instance. However, for historical analysis of campaign performance, ROMI is still a very useful metric to understand the profit generated by marketing communications.

STIMULATING SOCIAL CHANGE

TWO CASE STUDIES

Advertising isn't just a commercial tool, it is also a powerful driver of social change; and it can save taxpayers money. As John Fanning points out in his study *I Must be Talking to My Friends*,[86] there are many case studies that show how government advertising adds to, rather than diminishes, the public purse. Public sector advertising has been instrumental in influencing positive change in societies around the world by encouraging us to wear seat-belts, stop drink-driving, recycle household waste, give blood, reduce speeding and quit smoking. We will take a look now at two case studies from Ireland that clearly demonstrate the influence of this kind of advertising.

[86] Fanning, *I Must Be Talking to My Friends*, pg 71.

CASE STUDY

QUIT SMOKING

Smoking is a considerable burden on the Irish health service; half of all smokers die from tobacco-related illnesses and 90% of lung cancer cases are attributed to smoking.[87] Although the number of people using tobacco in Ireland had been declining over the years, almost three out of ten people were still smoking in 2011. Something significant needed to be done. A major new campaign was launched that year, which ran for four years, in two phases. The advertising focused on a key research finding - *one in every two smokers dies from a tobacco-related illness*. This is a shocking fact, but the real power of the campaign came from the emotion it stirred in people due to the true stories told by three real people: Gerry Collins an ex-smoker, Pauline Bell whose husband died from a tobacco-related heart attack and Margaret O'Brien who lost her mother to lung cancer.[88]

Gerry Collins would have the greatest impact on the nation. In the 2011 phase of the campaign Gerry spoke about how he had been diagnosed with throat cancer in 2008 and survived. The campaign was a great success and Gerry's life was returning to normal, but then, tragically, two years later, he discovered that he had terminal lung cancer and was given eight months to live. Gerry contacted the Health Service Executive in Ireland (HSE) to ask if he could take part in a new phase of the campaign that he hoped would inspire people to quit.

FIGURE 5.1: 48-SHEET POSTER

[87] HSE. *Smoking - The Facts*. Ireland: Health Service Executive. 2016.
[88] Cawley Nea\TBWA and Mediavest. *HSE QUIT*. ADFX Databank. 2012.

Three very moving commercials were shot with a brave and charismatic Gerry Collins sharing his thoughts about smoking, dying and his gratitude for his family and friends. He died on March 2nd 2014, shortly after the commercials were made.

Across the two phases of this extraordinary campaign, from 2011 to 2014, it is estimated that half of all smokers exposed to the campaign attempted to quit smoking as a result of the advertising - a staggering figure.[89]

A Eurobarometer survey showed that smoking rates fell faster in Ireland than in any other country in the EU during that time. In fact, tobacco use in Ireland had declined four times faster than the EU average, from 29% of adults in 2012 to 21% in 2014.[90]

Smoking costs the Irish health service up to €747 million per annum.[91] Although only a small portion (5%) of people who attempt to quit remain smoke-free, it is estimated that this campaign has saved the State an impressive €21.2 million[92 & 93] by reducing the number of smokers who will be a burden on the system.

FIGURE 5.2: PRESS ADVERTISEMENT

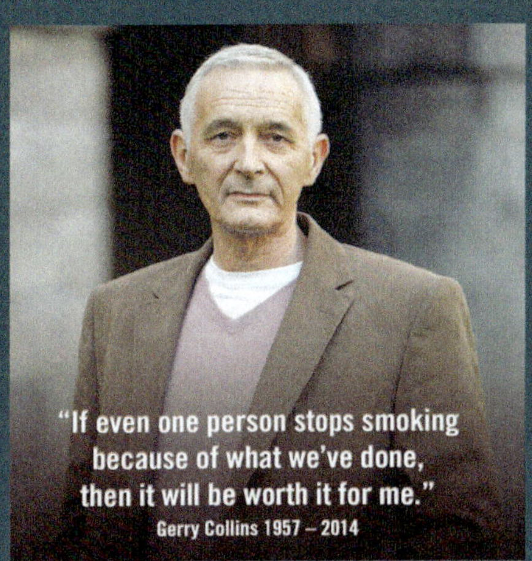

It is estimated that half of all smokers exposed to the campaign attempted to quit smoking as a result of the advertising

Agencies: Cawley Nea\TBWA & Mediavest & Carat

89 Cawley Nea\TBWA and Carat. *HSE QUIT 2*. ADFX Databank. 2014.
90 Cullen, Paul. *Irish Smoking Rates Falling Fastest in EU, Says Survey*. The Irish Times. 2015.
91 Cawley Nea\TBWA and Mediavest, *HSE QUIT*, pg 86.
92 Ibid.
93 Cawley Nea\TBWA and Carat, *HSE QUIT 2*.

CASE STUDY

DEPARTMENT OF THE ENVIRONMENT (NI) AND ROAD SAFETY AUTHORITY (ROI)

This case study describes how a long-term marketing communications campaign had a major impact on increasing seatbelt usage across the Republic of Ireland (ROI) and Northern Ireland (NI), thereby saving lives in both parts of the island, while providing an economic benefit to the taxpayer. The campaign was devised as a cross-border initiative, jointly commissioned by the respective statutory bodies, the Road Safety Authority in ROI and the Department of the Environment in NI.

Prior to the campaign, seatbelt compliance was weak in Ireland compared to European norms, particularly in ROI, and even more particularly in relation to rear seatbelt compliance. Seatbelt wearing rates for drivers were 55% in ROI and 87% in NI. Rear seatbelt usage was a deplorable 20% in ROI and 65% in NI.[94 & 95]

This deficit in seatbelt compliance was clearly linked, by statistical evidence, to higher death and serious injury rates in collisions. An advertising strategy was required to address this deviant behaviour by shifting attitudes and behaviours. Advertising agency, LyleBailie, was retained to create a campaign using techniques drawn from neuroscience and psychology to embed emotional memory to influence seatbelt wearing decisions.

The first creative treatment, *Damage*, was launched in 2001. It used shocking imagery to communicate that brain damage and death are the outcomes of not wearing a seatbelt in a collision. This was backed up with the tagline *No Seatbelt - No Excuse*.

94 RSA. *Seatbelt Observational Study*. Ireland: Road Safety Authority. 1999.
95 Department of the Environment. *Northern Ireland Seatbelt Survey*. 2000.

Two further extensions of the core idea were added in 2006. *Selfish* persuaded parents that the most selfish thing they can do is to allow their children travel unrestrained, whereas *Get it On* reinforced, to younger rear seat passengers, that not wearing a seatbelt has consequences beyond themselves.

FIGURE 5.3: IMAGES FROM *DAMAGE* TELEVISION COMMERCIAL

The campaign, which ran between 2001 and 2007, achieved both attitudinal improvements and behavioural change, resulting in significant increases in seatbelt wearing rates, with a reduction in death and serious injuries.

It is estimated that the advertising delivered a direct economic benefit of £66.3 million due to the lives it was responsible for saving

Driver wearing rates in NI went from being the lowest to the highest in the UK, increasing to 95%. Back-seat compliance increased to 90%. In the Republic of Ireland (ROI), driver usage increased to 88% and back-seat wearing quadrupled to 84%. During the six years before the campaign, 2,840 people were killed or seriously injured while not wearing a seatbelt in ROI and NI. In the six years after the campaign began, the number of deaths and serious injuries fell to 1,708. It is estimated that the advertising delivered a direct economic benefit of £66.3 million due to the lives it was responsible for saving.[96]

Agency: LyleBailie International

[96] Lyle, David, et al. *Department of the Environment (NI) and Road Safety Authority (ROI) – The Longer-Term Effects of Seatbelt Advertising 2001-2007.* Warc. 2008.

CHAPTER 6

ECONOMETRICS EXPLAINED BY JENNIFER CRUISE

Econometrics is a discipline concerned with mathematically modelling economic and social phenomena; it is predicated on the notion that, underlying the apparent randomness and disorder of events that we observe, there is a set of regular and invariant structures that determine these events. The hypothesis is that any statistical phenomenon, e.g., GDP, population growth, sales, footfall, website visits, etc., is composed of a determinate and random component, and that even the random component has its own regularities.

The work of the econometrician is to identify these deterministic factors and build a mathematical equation that will explain the phenomenon of interest, e.g., sales.

Econometrics has its origins in the work of Francis Galton, a Victorian scientist and cousin of Charles Darwin. His 1869 book *Hereditary Genius*[97] investigated how and why intellectual, physical and personality traits run in families. In the proceeding 150 years there have been seismic advances in the field; improved statistical techniques, computing power and most recently an explosion of data. Governments, banks and corporations have adopted econometrics to understand the past and assist in forecasting the future.

[97] Galton, Francis. *Hereditary Genius: An inquiry Into its Laws and Consequences.* Macmillan, 1869.

One notably mature application of econometrics has been in the measurement of advertising and marketing effectiveness. For almost sixty years, econometrics has been employed by organisations to model their sales curves and, in doing so, isolate and quantify the role played by advertising and marketing activities. Investment in econometrics gives immediate guidance on how to grow profit, properly evaluate marketing performance and make evidence-based decisions.

Econometric modelling identifies the factors driving sales and quantifies their effects. This allows organisations to evaluate the historical return on marketing investment of factors as wide ranging as TV advertising, promotions, the weather, the economy and competitor communications, to name a few. In fact, it can measure the contribution of any variable that has a role in driving sales of a product or service. It can also use this information to predict future sales.

So, how does the process work and what steps are involved in building an econometric model?

The first stage should be a deep dive session with the econometrician, to ensure he/she is fully briefed on the business in question, its competitor landscape, consumer trends and to learn unique insight and perspective about the business from the marketer. It is also recommended that the econometrician engages with the relevant marketing communication agencies to get an understanding of the strategy, execution and observed performance to date. The technical process of building and interpreting the model can take six to twelve weeks, during which time a clear and open line of communication should exist between the econometrician and key stakeholders to validate findings, explain anomalies and ensure results are logically grounded.

No two businesses are the same and, as a result, no two econometric models ever are either. However, there are common stages that should be followed throughout the course of any project, which can largely be grouped into seven distinct phases.

FIGURE 6.1: SEVEN PHASES OF AN ECONOMETRIC PROJECT

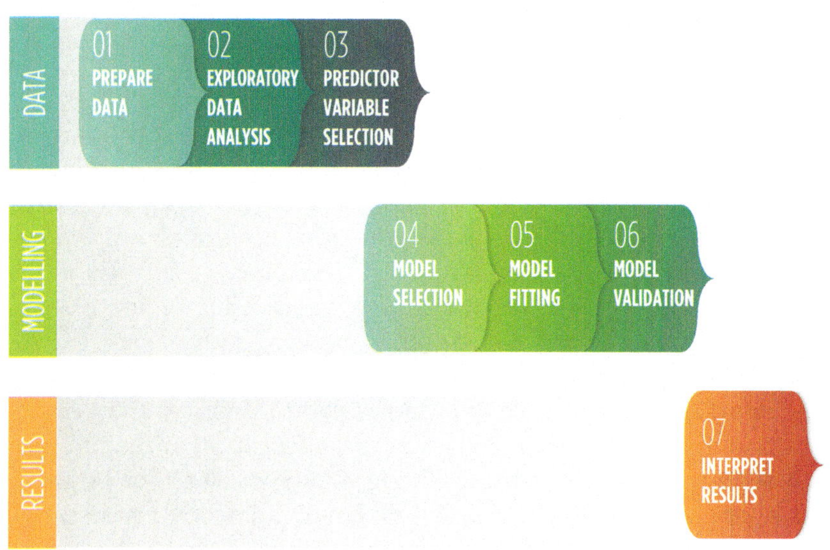

The first step can be one of the most time consuming phases, because it involves the collation of all data pertinent to explaining the sales curve. This can be a challenge for some companies, but a lot of the information required is readily available via third party providers. A minimum of two years of data should be provided, as this enables the modeller to identify seasonal factors. The data must be provided weekly, i.e., 104 weeks of data for two years; monthly data is generally too broad and hides variations from week to week that the model needs to see. Typical data sets required include advertising exposure by week, sales revenue, pricing, trade promotions, weather, changes in distribution, economic data, incidence of major sporting or cultural events and even PR exposure. The data are not just required for the brands being modelled; competitor data are also required, where possible.

Step two is the exploratory data analysis phase and is a critical step in the process. This is where the econometrician investigates the data to identify trends, patterns, seasonality and relationships between different variables and how they influence or are related to sales.

Econometrics can measure the contribution of any variable that has a role in driving sales

Step three identifies the variables with the greatest predictive power. In addition to using exploratory analysis for predictor variable selection, econometricians will also use numerous statistical techniques such as *principal component analysis* and *factor analysis*. It may also be necessary at this stage to lag certain variables; for instance an economic indicator like consumer sentiment may need to be lagged by three to six months to understand the impact it has on sales with longer purchase lead-in times, like cars. Other variables may need to be transformed to reflect their manifestation in reality. For example, a TV campaign will have a carryover effect beyond the weeks of transmission; established ad-stock techniques will be applied at this stage to ensure that the decayed impact of that activity is represented in the data.

Steps four through six are where the model is created. The econometrician will generally apply multiple modelling techniques; *linear, generalised linear, local nested regression* and *structured equation modelling* are just some of the techniques at their disposal. Each iteration of the model should be fitted to data and validated until the optimal model is built. There are numerous statistical tests that the econometrician will use to measure the accuracy and fit of each iteration, but of equal importance during the selection stage is the logical fit: does it make common sense and does it mirror reality?

Once the final model is built, the econometrician will move into the final step, which is the interpretation phase. This is where the model is decomposed into all of its component variables and the influence that each variable had over the period under investigation can then be quantified and visualised; like un-baking a cake into its ingredients. At that stage, outputs like the chart below are created showing what percentage of sales revenue is driven by media (versus the natural revenue base) and how the media element is broken down by type.

FIGURE 6.2: EXAMPLE OF AN OUTPUT FROM AN ECONOMETRIC MODEL

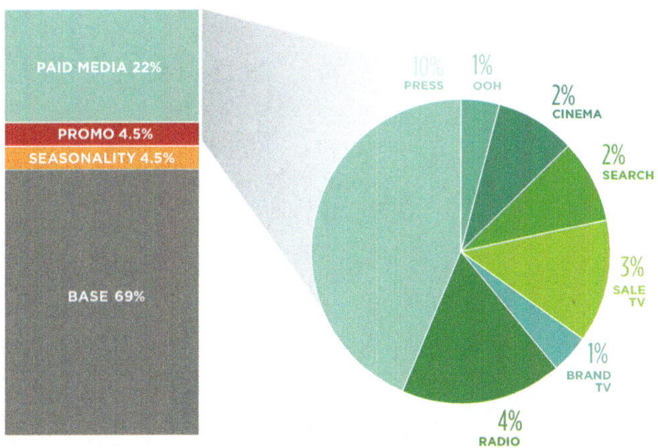

Note: For illustrative purposes only

Furthermore, by layering in spend across all media elements, a measure of the *revenue returned on marketing investment* can be calculated and, crucially, the *profit returned on marketing investment*. The latter can only be calculated if the econometrician is provided with the necessary profit margin equation and it is very important that this is forthcoming, otherwise the true return on investment cannot be established. Equipped with this information, projected response curves can be created for each element of the media budget, which demonstrate how revenue and profit would grow as investment in that medium increases (see Chapter 7). The point of diminishing returns can also be established. This information can then be applied to budget setting and optimisation for future activity.

In addition to understanding the performance of each medium in isolation, the outputs of an advanced econometrics project can also help explain the interplay across the entire media ecosystem – how each channel affects and supports the other. In the example below, 22% of sales were driven by paid media. The solid lines indicate the direct role each channel played in driving sales, while the dotted lines show how each touchpoint assisted in the process. The size of each bubble is reflective of the value contributed by each channel.

FIGURE 6.3: EXAMPLE OF AN OUTPUT FROM AN ADVANCED ECONOMETRIC MODEL

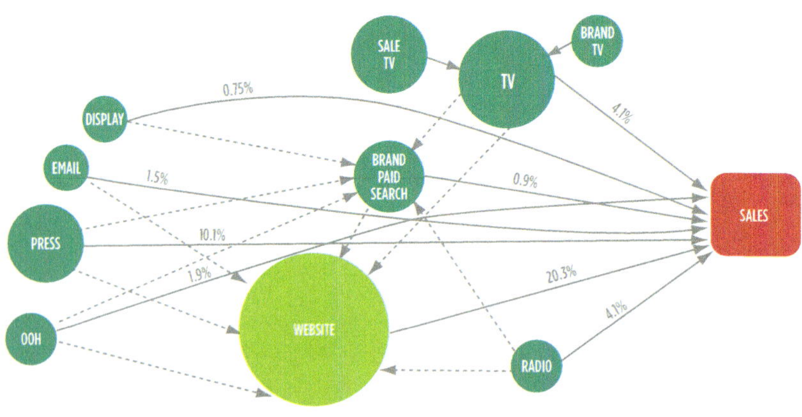

Note: For illustrative purposes only

This type of analysis uncovers direct and indirect drivers of business performance, which allows the media mix to be truly optimised.

We are seeing a marked shift in the evolution of econometrics due to advances in technology and data exchange; it is now possible to continuously update and optimise models seamlessly by establishing direct links to data sources.

Econometricians can fine-tune models at fixed intervals to react to economic and market changes. Marketers and agencies can have access to results in near real-time via online visualisation portals and the outputs from the model can be used to inform planning at a much more granular level. Likewise, as econometricians embrace the expanding field of data science they are able to bring new levels of insight and investigation to their studies, such as understanding consumer segments, retention and churn drivers.

The benefits to the marketer can be enormous; an integrated analytics approach can free up between 15% and 20% of marketing spending.[98]

[98] Bhandari, Rishi et al. *Using Marketing Analytics to Drive Superior Growth*. June 2014.

The next great frontier for econometrics will be its marriage with programmatic buying platforms, i.e., the creation of parallel, dynamic sales response curves that can calculate the expected return from each piece of inventory, depending on the characteristics of the audience, medium and context.

> Marketers and agencies can have access to results in near real-time via online visualisation portals

This will not only determine the optimum portfolio of inventory to purchase, but set the price based on expected return.

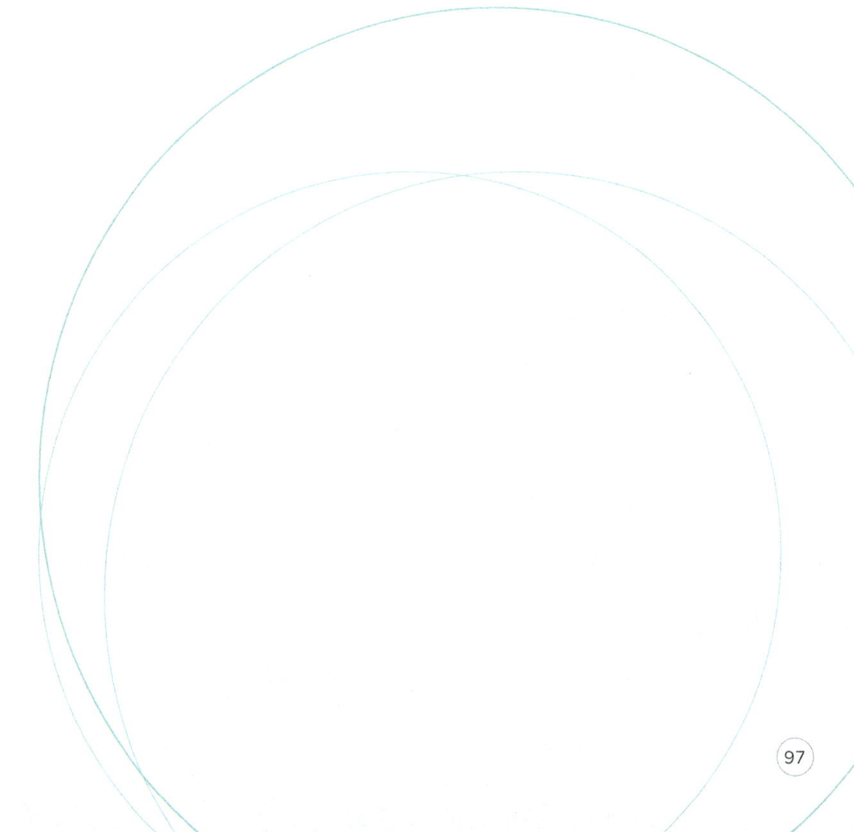

CHAPTER 7

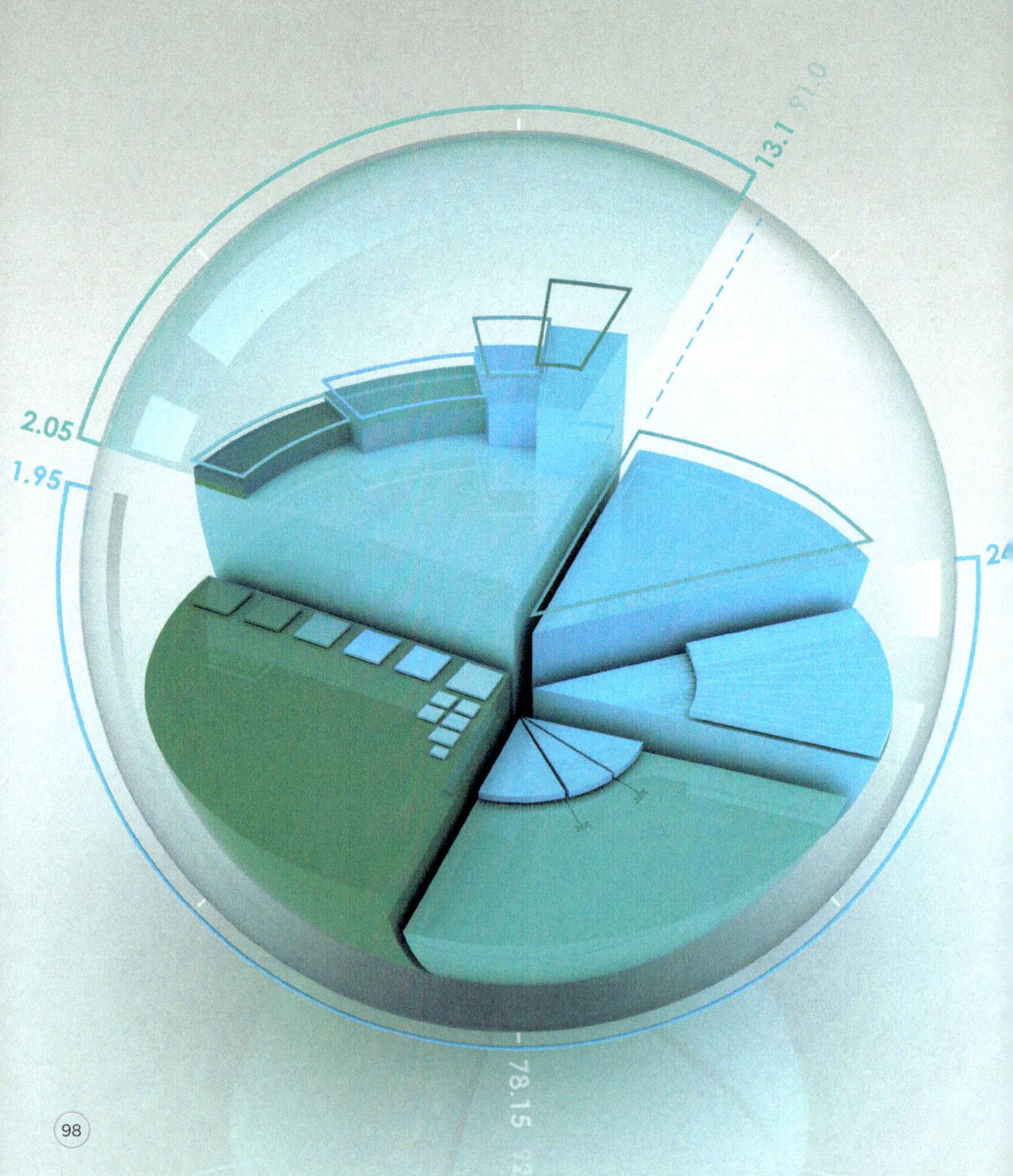

SETTING A BUDGET

Global advertising expenditure reached $542 billion in 2016.[99] The purpose of this massive economic investment is to stimulate demand and generate growth. The allocation of these resources is a great responsibility; it is imperative that they are deployed optimally through a scientific process.

Many methods are used to set budgets for marketing communications; quite a common technique is to allocate a fixed percentage of sales to the task. Often, a company will allocate what they believe is 'affordable' to the business. In other cases, a firm may simply apply the previous year's budget plus inflation.

> 'Unhealthy brands' tend to set their advertising budget as an almost constant percentage of sales

A 2016 study by Abas Mirzaei et al.[100] found that *'unhealthy brands'* tend to set their advertising budget as an almost constant percentage of sales; they also tend to spend less on advertising and do so in a haphazard manner. The report went on to say that such brands are very vulnerable to market threats and competitors' strategies. The authors advise that poor-performing brands need to develop long-term advertising-spending strategies that *'gently and regularly'* increase investment relative to competitors. Consistency in how the budget is deployed is essential if any significant improvement in brand health is to be achieved.[100]

[99] Austin et al., *Zenith Advertising Expenditure Forecast*, pg 16.

[100] Mirzaei, Abas et al. *Assessing Ad-Spend Patterns to Predict Brand Health: A Model for Advertisers to Determine Future Advertising-Budgeting Strategies*. Journal of Advertising Research, 56(2). April 2016.

The key problem with the way budgets are generally allocated is that they do not follow scientific or evidence-based techniques. Also, they tend *not* to be geared to the specific business challenge being faced by the brand.

> Consistency in how the budget is deployed is essential if any significant improvement in brand health is to be achieved

However, there is a growing trend towards the use of econometric modelling by marketers. As described in the last chapter, this *is* a scientific process that uses mathematical models to measure past marketing activity to improve future marketing effectiveness (see Chapter 6). One of its key outputs is to establish the correct level of budget to achieve a commercial objective.

FIGURE 7.1: RESPONSE CURVES THAT SHOW REVENUE & PROFIT FOR DIFFERENT LEVELS OF INVESTMENT

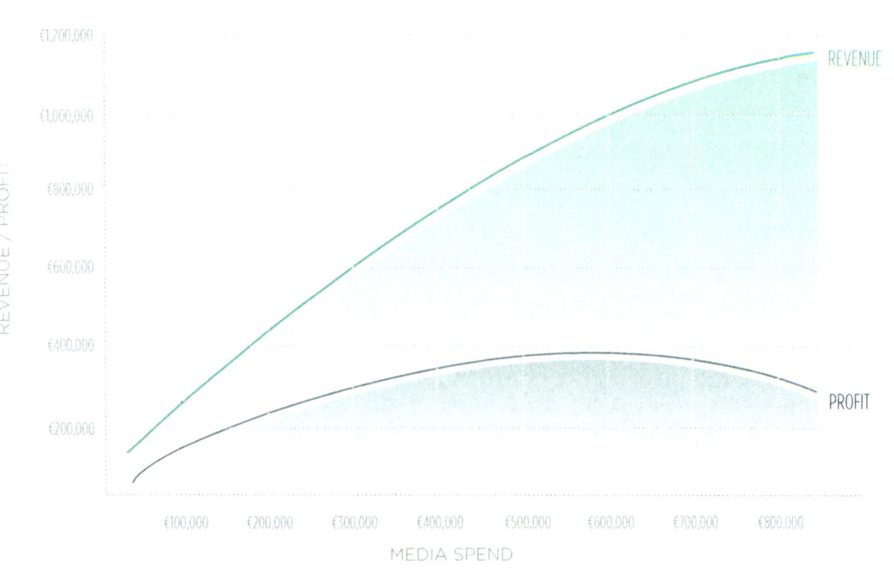

Note: for illustrative purposes only

The process generates a response curve (see Figure 7.1), which enables practitioners to forecast revenue and profit for different levels of investment in marketing communications. Saturation levels of investment for each marketing channel can also be identified. This, in turn, drives an optimisation tool, which calculates the impact of different budget levels and media combinations to arrive at the ideal level of investment for the campaign in question (see Figure 7.2).

FIGURE 7.2: CORE OPTIMISATION TOOL

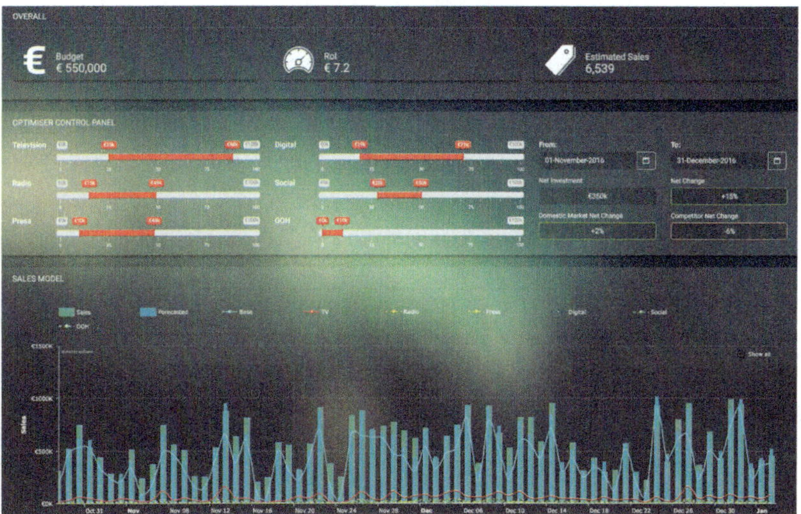

Econometric modelling is often called the gold standard of budget setting, but it does have a key limitation; it is based on historical information. This is an obvious problem for brands that have no history on which to base their budget decisions.

> Share of voice has proven to be a stronger measure than absolute spend for budget setting

This brings us to an alternative, reliable budget-setting method. It is based on the relationship between *share of voice* (SOV) and *share of market* (SOM). SOV has proven to be a stronger measure than absolute spend for budget setting, because it factors in the competitiveness of the category.

There is a large body of evidence available to prove that when a brand invests ahead of its market share, it generally experiences growth. In other words, when a brand's SOV is greater than its SOM it is more likely to gain market share. The crucial measure of this phenomenon is *extra share of voice* (ESOV). ESOV is essentially the difference between the brand's *share of voice* (i.e., share of category communications expenditure across all channels) and its *share of market*.

Research studies, carried out over many years, across hundreds of brands, have established a strong relationship between ESOV and market share growth.

When a brand's share of voice is greater than its share of market, it is more likely to gain market share

The starting point in the budget setting process is to establish the brand's equilibrium position; this is the point at which it should expect to maintain its existing market share. The standard principle is that a brand is in a state of equilibrium when its SOV is equal to its SOM. However, where possible, this should be modelled for the category, because the relationship between these two metrics is not always linear. Brand size can, and usually does, have an impact.

None of this is new; James O. Peckham first wrote about the relationship between SOV and SOM in the 1970s[101] and many studies have supported its importance ever since, including research carried out by Simon Broadbent (1989),[102] John Philip Jones (1990)[103] and Stephan Buck (2001)[104]. More recently, extensive research into the topic has been carried out by Les Binet and Peter Field (2007);[105] they established important new benchmarks for budget setting and provided evidence to show that the relationship between SOV and SOM varies according to the nature of the brand and the market it's operating in.

101 Peckham, James O. *The Wheel of Marketing*. 1973.
102 Broadbent, Simon. *The Advertising Budget: The Advertiser's Guide to Budget Determination*. McGraw-Hill. 1989.
103 Jones. *Ad Spending*, pg 12.
104 Buck, Stephan. *The True Cost of Cutting Ad-Spend*. Warc. 2001.
105 Binet and Field, *Marketing in the Era of Accountability*, pg 12.

Figure 7.3 below shows a good correlation between share growth (vertical axis) and ESOV (horizontal axis) for the 127 cases analysed by Binet and Field.[106] The bigger the ESOV, the faster a brand's market share tends to grow.

The reverse is also true; if a brand has negative ESOV, it is likely to lose market share in a similar proportion. Ideally, value market share (as opposed to volume) should be used, as it includes the effect of relative pricing.[107]

FIGURE 7.3: EXTRA SHARE OF VOICE (ESOV) VERSUS MARKET SHARE GROWTH

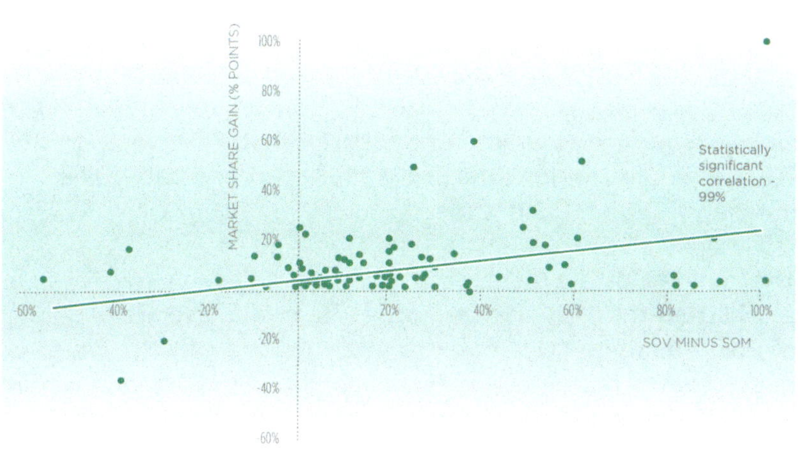

Binet and Field found that, on average, every ten points of ESOV generates 2.2 percentage points of extra market share growth. However, this study focused on high-performing campaigns from the IPA Effectiveness Awards database, which are not typical of average, everyday campaigns. To account for this, Binet and Field conducted further analysis to extrapolate from the IPA data an industry-wide relationship between growth and ESOV. This analysis suggested that, for an average campaign, ten points of ESOV generates around one point of extra share growth, about half that of the IPA-grade cases.[108]

106 Nielsen and IPA, *How Share of Voice Wins Market Share*, pg 12.
107 Binet and Field, *Marketing in the Era of Accountability*, pg 12.
108 Ibid.

Binet and Field were able to show how this varied across different sectors. For example, they noted that the *fast-moving consumer goods* (FMCG) sector was much less responsive to ESOV than *services* and *durables*. Their estimation for a typical FMCG brand was 0.3 points of growth per ten points of ESOV.

> For an average campaign, ten points of ESOV generates around one point of extra share growth

The industry was curious to have this corroborated through analysis of a more broadly based dataset. Therefore, the IPA commissioned a new study in 2009, *How Share of Voice Wins Market Share*, to validate (or disprove) the findings of the 2007 Binet and Field work, using a fully representative Nielsen dataset of 123 FMCG brands.[109]

The new study validated the Binet and Field work. Nielsen established that, for an average FMCG brand, every ten points of ESOV leads to 0.5% of extra market share growth, which is quite close to the Binet and Field estimation of 0.3% and within the statistical margin of error.[110]

While SOV/SOM analysis is a highly recommended starting point for budget setting, it is important to also layer in other factors that will influence the budget such as brand size, market category, product life stage and campaign quality. The 2009 analysis conducted by Nielsen corroborated Binet and Field's findings in relation to brand size; Nielsen found that, on average, brand leaders achieved 1.4% of share growth per ten percentage points of ESOV, compared to 0.4% for challenger brands. Therefore, a typical FMCG challenger needs to be at least three and a half times as effective as the leader to compete.[111]

[109] Nielsen and IPA, *How Share of Voice Wins Market Share*, pg 12.
[110] Ibid.
[111] Ibid.

Furthermore, the Nielsen research showed that brands with market share levels of over 10% achieved on average around two and a half times the level of share growth per point of ESOV than brands with market share levels of under 10%. A key reason for the difference is that larger brands have distribution, range and pricing to help to maintain and increase share.

Research from John Philip Jones is consistent with this; he found that brands with market share in excess of 25% could maintain their position with a SOV that was 5% lower than market share, whereas brands with less than 10% market share needed SOV around 4% above market share to *'hold their own.'* [112] Nielsen also found that 'new news' is another important distinguishing factor in campaign performance, meaning that brand launches or relaunches typically achieved 15-25% greater growth per point of ESOV than the norm.[113]

A recent study into this topic by Karen Hand and Jill McGrath (2015) verifies the findings from previous studies. Hand and McGrath examined 106 cases from the IAPI ADFX awards databank in Ireland. They found that the change in value market share was 1.8 for every ten percentage points of ESOV, which is broadly in line with the Binet and Field (2007) finding of 2.2.[114]

In summary, the weight of evidence in support of the relationship between SOV and SOM is compelling. The lack of complexity to the methodology sometimes causes suspicion among marketers, but the scientific analysis of hundreds of case studies has ensured that this correlation is now a well-established fact. It is an excellent guide for marketers in budget setting and provides all the ammunition necessary to build a strong business case to their boards. Moreover, the relationship between ESOV and growth has remained consistent despite the changing nature of the media landscape. It is as relevant now, in the age of social media as it was twenty years ago.

112 Jones, *Ad Spending*, pg 12.
113 Nielsen and IPA, *How Share of Voice Wins Market Share*, pg 12.
114 Hand and McGrath, *A Line in the Sand*, pg 71.

CHAPTER 8

SHORT-TERM THINKING REDUCES PROFIT

A legacy of the financial crisis that rocked the world in 2008, and led to the deepest global recession since the Great Depression, has been the significant growth in short-termism in many aspects of commerce. While the true effect of this issue is usually difficult to isolate, its impact on brand and profit growth can be clearly seen, thanks to the work of Peter Field in his study *Selling Creativity Short*[115] and in the latest work he carried out with his long-time collaborator, Les Binet, for *Marketing in The Digital Age*,[116] both commissioned by the IPA (UK). The extent of the rise in short-term marketing campaigns is worrying, as can be seen in Figure 8.1. These data relate to cases contained in the IPA Databank (in the UK), but it is widely believed to be an international issue.

FIGURE 8.1: THE SHIFT IN THE IPA DATABANK TOWARDS SHORT-TERM CAMPAIGNS

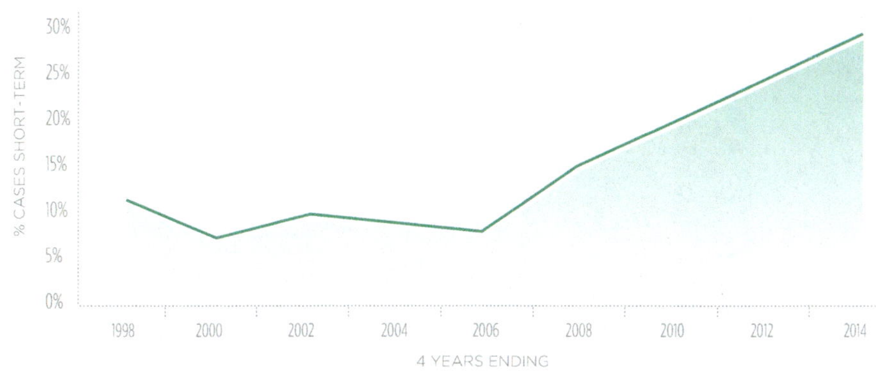

[115] Field, *Selling Creativity Short*, pg 11.
[116] Binet and Field, *Marketing in the Digital Age*, pg 13.

Since 2006, the percentage of IPA case studies that are short-term in nature (i.e., less than six months in duration) has more than quadrupled to over 30%,[117] - an extraordinary increase.

> Since 2006, the percentage of short-term campaigns has more than quadrupled

This shift has been a result of recession-driven urgency in businesses to build immediate sales, and a consensus among senior management that success will be achieved through short-term tactics, rather than long-term brand-building strategies. What complicates the situation is that their intuition is partly correct; this is why it is so dangerous. Short-term initiatives are, in fact, more effective at driving sales effects in the short-term, but long-term campaigns (those that are evaluated over periods of longer than six months) are around three times more efficient in growing market share.[118] Figure 8.2, taken from *Selling Creativity Short*, provides a clear analysis of the strengths and weaknesses of both approaches.

FIGURE 8.2: LINK BETWEEN CAMPAIGN DURATION AND EFFECTIVENESS

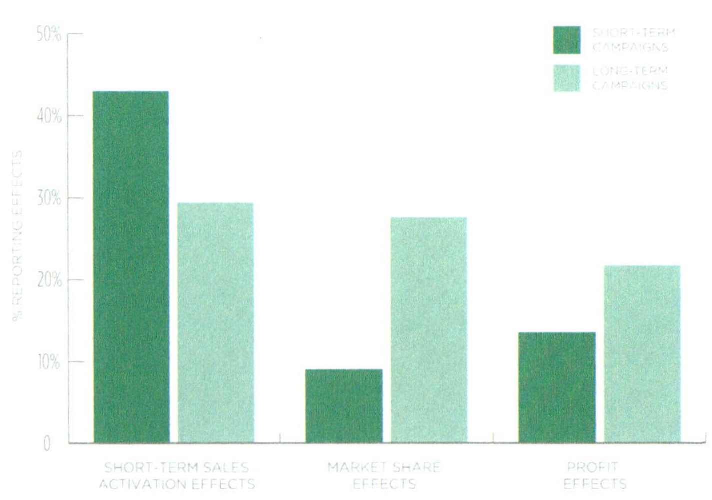

[117] Field, *Selling Creativity Short*, pg 11.
[118] Ibid.

The problem is that much of the thinking at senior management level has gone like this: *'As long as our annual plan is filled with activity designed to drive immediate sales, then we are optimising the use of our budget.'* Unfortunately, the evidence contradicts this belief. A quote from the famous management consultant, Peter Drucker, referred to in *Selling Creativity Short*, sums up the short-termism problem:

'This means damaging, if not destroying, the wealth-producing capacity of the business...Long-term results cannot be achieved by piling short-term results on short-term results.'[119]

Interestingly, the availability of real-time analytics regarding the effect of marketing activities in digital media, is fuelling this obsession with short-termism. To be clear, there is nothing wrong with engaging in short-term marketing initiatives; the problem is that this must be balanced with long-term strategies in order to deliver the optimum result in terms of profit.

Long-term campaigns are three times more efficient in growing market share, than short-term campaigns

[119] Drucker, Peter F. *Post Capitalist Society*. Harper Information. 1993.

60:40 RATIO

Binet and Field first reported the concept of a 60:40 ratio of long-term brand-building (broad reach, emotional creative) and short-term sales activation (tightly targeted and information rich) in their 2007 report *Marketing in the Era of Accountability*.[120]

Their contention (based on analysis of the IPA databank of case studies) is that, on average, brands should spend 60% of their budget on brand-building activity and 40% on activation, because this ratio delivers maximum efficiency and maximum effectiveness.

The 60:40 ratio is a rule of thumb and varies by category. Binet and Field revisited it in 2013 and again in 2016 and found that the ratio still holds true. However, it should not be assumed that this will be the correct split in every case. It is important to establish the optimum ratio for each brand; ideally, this should be done using econometric modelling.

But the market does not appear to be heeding this scientific proof and worrying trends have emerged that are resulting in a growing underperformance of marketing. Firstly, the percentage of marketing communications budgets being spent on activation now exceeds the optimum (based on UK IPA data), increasing from 31% in 2014 to 47% in 2016.[121]

Brands should spend 60% of their budget on brand-building activity and 40% on activation

120 Binet and Field, *Marketing in the Era of Accountability*, pg 12.
121 Clift, Joseph. *Marketing in the Digital Age: Binet and Field on How Media Choices Impact Effectiveness*. Warc. 2016.

This has been compounded by falling budgets; since 2006, average IPA case study budgets, expressed as *extra share of voice* (ESOV), have fallen by around twelve percentage points. For creatively-awarded campaigns, the fall has been even greater, at around twenty percentage points, taking them into negative ESOV territory for the first time in the twenty-year run of data (see Figure 8.3).[122]

As described earlier in this book, ESOV is the difference between the brand's *share of voice* (i.e., share of category communications expenditure across all channels) and its *share of market*. It is used here, because it provides a level playing field on which to compare campaigns with very different expenditure levels.

FIGURE 8.3: THE DECLINE IN BUDGETS SEEN IN THE IPA DATABANK

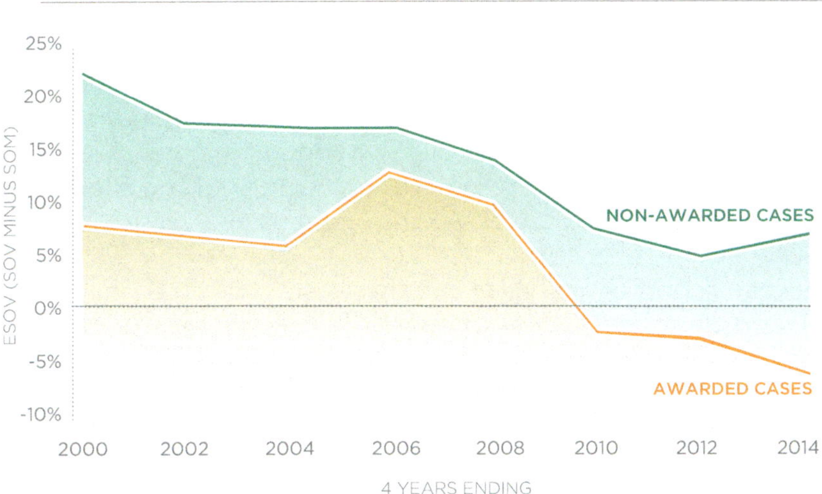

The decline in investment in marketing communications, particularly for the creatively-awarded cases, suggests that marketers are expecting their creative work to offset the impact of declining budgets, by the campaigns *'punching above their weight'*. The data clearly show that this doesn't work in the vast majority of cases and that investment in creativity can be wasted by a lack of sufficient media exposure.

122 Field, *Selling Creativity Short*, pg 11.

The research concludes that growth is achieved through a combination of effective advertising and strong investment in media space/time. Negative ESOV eliminates the benefits of creativity. Investment in marketing communications needs to be in positive ESOV territory to drive sustainable growth in market share.

We must note here that a significant part of the problem is the PLC quarterly reporting cycle, which drives management to focus excessively on short-term performance, thus distracting them from long-term growth strategies.

In 2013, McKinsey and the Canada Pension Plan Investment Board (CPPID) conducted a survey of 1,000 board members and C-level executives around the world to assess their progress in taking a longer-term approach to running their companies.

86% of respondents said that using a longer time horizon to make business decisions would positively affect corporate performance by strengthening financial returns and increasing innovation. However, 79% felt pressurised to demonstrate strong financial performance over a period of just two years or less, and 63% said the pressure to generate strong short-term results had increased over the previous five years.[123]

The joint report of McKinsey and the CPPID, published in the Harvard Business Review, ponders the reasons for this gap between knowing the right thing to do and actually doing it. The obvious answer is the continuing pressure on public companies from financial markets to maximise short-term results. Respondents to the study made it clear that they were often just channelling increased short-term pressures from investors, including institutional shareholders.

Encouragingly, Europe scrapped mandatory quarterly reporting at the end of 2014, citing the pressure it places on smaller companies and its encouragement of short-term thinking. However, many companies continue to publish quarterly results.

[123] Barton, Dominic and Wiseman, Mark. *Focusing Capital on the Long Term*. Harvard Business Review. January - February 2014

Since the removal of the obligation in December 2014, only 30 FTSE 100 companies and 139 FTSE 250 companies have stopped publishing quarterly reports (as of 5th October 2016).[124] In November 2016 the Investment Association called on all companies in the UK to follow suit. Its statement read:

'We call for companies to cease reporting quarterly and refocus reporting on a broader range of strategic issues. Companies should focus on improvements in reporting on the long-term drivers of sustainable value creation and shift resources towards improved reporting on long-term strategy and capital management.'[125]

This is encouraging, but the philosophy needs to spread beyond Europe. At the time of writing, there is still no change on the horizon in the United States where all public companies must file quarterly reports.

> A significant part of the problem is the PLC quarterly reporting cycle, which drives management to focus excessively on short-term performance, thus distracting them from long-term growth strategies

124 The Investment Association UK. *Public Position Statement: Quarterly Reporting and Quarterly Earnings Guidance*. November 2016.
125 Ibid.

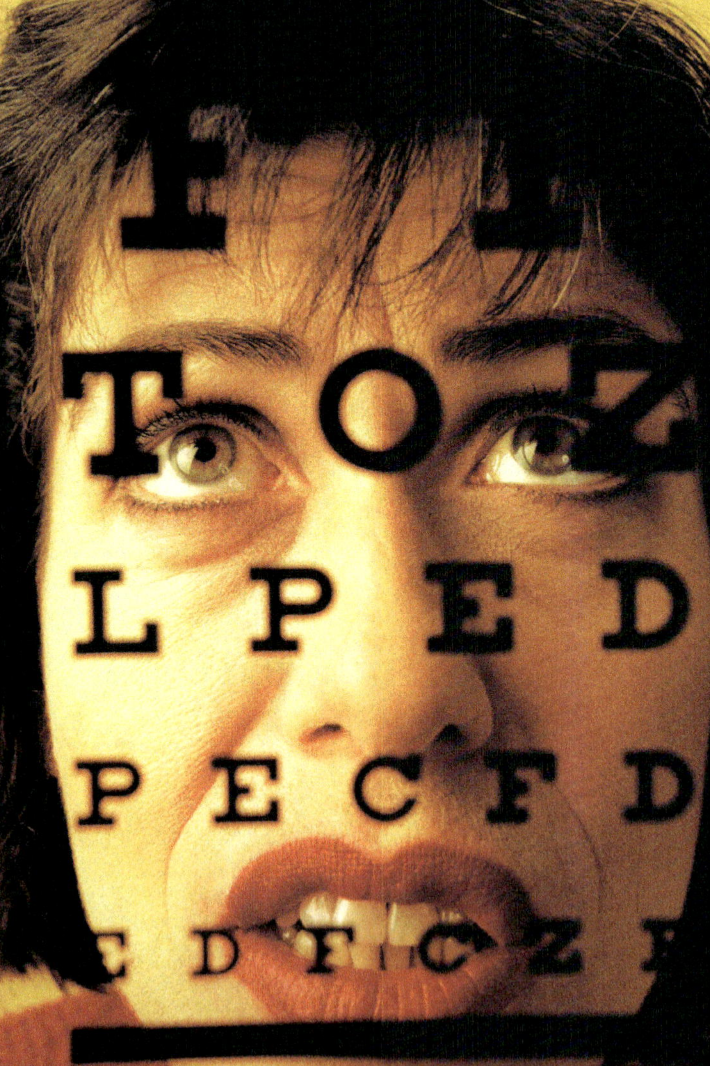
E
T O Z
L P E D
P E C F D

THE POWER OF LONG-TERM THINKING

A CASE STUDY

CASE STUDY

SPECSAVERS

This Specsavers case study provides compelling evidence of the ability of marketing communications to be an engine of growth for businesses. This is the story of a company that was launched in 1984 and grew to a major international success.

Specsavers invested circa £500 million in advertising between 1984 and 2013.[126] Through a consistent strategy, and a commanding *share of voice*, it has achieved considerable revenue growth and a dominant market share.

However, as we noted earlier in this book, it's not just the volume of money deployed that counts; the most successful brands also believe in the power of creativity and invest accordingly. This company is no exception. *Should've gone to Specsavers* is a great example of a core idea that has stood the test of time. Not only has it achieved exceptionally high levels of recognition in the markets it serves, it also gave birth to likeable and entertaining advertising, which has warmed people to the brand over the years.

FIGURE 8.4: SPECSAVERS TV COMMERCIAL

[126] Philip, Matthew et al. *Should've Gone to Specsavers: A Far-Sighted View of Advertising's Role in Building a Business Over 30 Years*. Warc. 2014.

The current guise of *Should've gone to Specsavers* (running since 2008) has also been highly effective for the business; in fact, it is three times more efficient at driving revenue than any other marketing communications used by the company over the previous twenty years.[127]

Figure 8.6 shows the kind of analysis that advertising/ media agencies have used in the past to demonstrate the effectiveness of their work. It is a one dimensional correlation that overclaims the role of marketing communications and ignores other key variables, particularly store openings. Making claims based on analysis like this has probably been one of the factors that has driven the level of cynicism in boardrooms towards 'advertising people'.

FIGURE 8.5: SPECSAVERS 6-SHEET 'SPECIAL EDITION'

FIGURE 8.6: SPECSAVERS' REVENUE AND MEDIA SPEND

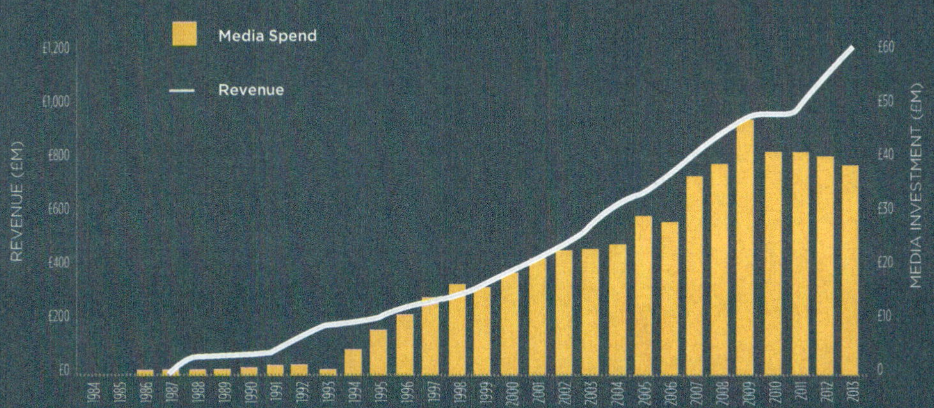

127 Philip, *Should've Gone to Specsavers*, pg 116.

However, in this case, Specsavers and its agency, Manning Gottlieb OMD, invested in ongoing econometric modelling to identify the key factors driving the revenue growth. This analysis quantified the contribution of all relevant variables and found that advertising investment and store growth were the most important (see Figure 8.7).[128]

FIGURE 8.7: KEY FACTORS DRIVING SPECSAVERS' REVENUE GROWTH

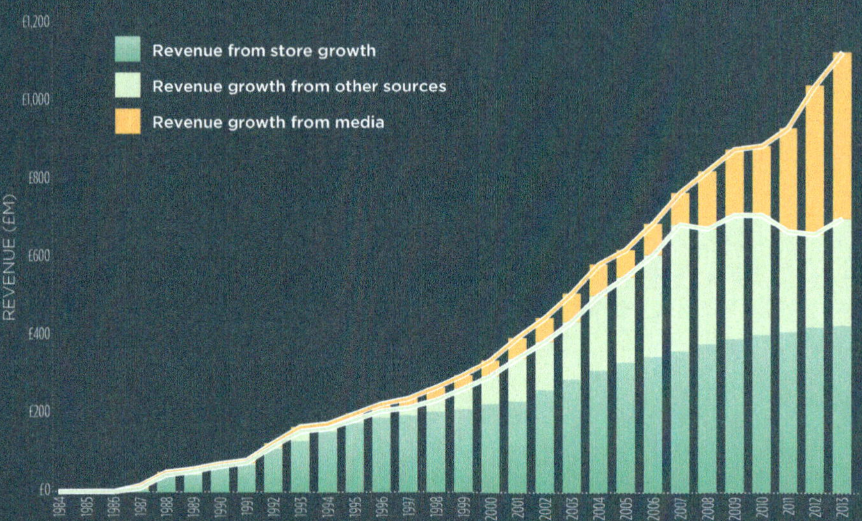

The other key factor in Specsavers' success is the consistency of its investment over time, despite changing market conditions and competitive pressures. This strategy of continuous presence at relatively high spend levels, combined with excellent creative work, has been directly responsible for the company delivering £2.1 billion in incremental revenue and an incremental net profit (from advertising) of £629.7 million over 30 years[129] (see Figure 8.8).

[128] Philip, *Should've Gone to Specsavers*, pg 116.
[129] Ibid.

FIGURE 8.8: ECONOMETRICS - RETURN ON INVESTMENT ANALYSIS

Incremental revenue driven by media	**£2,094,567,659**
Marginal contribution to profit	**53.3%**
Incremental profit driven by media	**£1,116,404,562**
Media spend	**£486,737,994**
Net profit	**£629,666,568**
Return on marketing investment	**129%**

This long-running campaign delivered £2.1 billion in incremental revenue and an incremental net profit of £629.7 million over 30 years

Agency: Manning Gottlieb OM

CHAPTER 9

EMOTIONAL CAMPAIGNS DRIVE MORE PROFIT

The John Lewis case study, which is featured after this chapter, clearly demonstrates the effectiveness of emotional advertising. However, it would be wrong to believe that this phenomenon is confined to soft, sentimental Christmas campaigns; research clearly shows that emotion in marketing communications is more effective than rational messaging over the long-term.

Rational campaigns do enjoy an advantage in relation to short-term direct effects, but this advantage is temporary. The key challenge for marketers is to know how to phase and weight both the emotional and rational elements of a marketing programme in order to establish the optimum blend between the two. We will return to this point at the end of the chapter.

First, what do we mean by 'emotional' marketing? This is advertising or other messaging that is designed to influence how consumers feel about brands (or issues), rather than how they think about them.[130] This is achieved by tapping into one or more of the primary emotions: surprise, sadness and joy (or sometimes anger, disgust and fear). This is one of the fourteen key marketing effectiveness concepts addressed by Binet and Field in their exhaustive analysis of the IPA databank of 880 cases studies, which they first reported in their 2007 study, *Marketing in the Era of Accountability*.[131]

[130] Field, *Selling Creativity Short*, pg 11.

[131] Binet and Field, *Marketing in the Era of Accountability*, pg 12.

'Emotional involvement campaigns,' they wrote, *'work by touching emotions or feelings in consumers...The intention is to transfer these emotions to the brand and consequently to build empathy in the consumer/brand relationship. Through empathy they seek to influence choice.'*[132]

Binet and Field's work is packed full of persuasive evidence to demonstrate that 'emotional' advertising is more likely to achieve better business results than 'rational' communications, which rely on information to persuade consumers. They found that emotionally-based campaigns outperform rationally-based campaigns on every business measure; they are significantly more profitable (see Figure 9.1), they are better at generating awareness, they are stronger at creating differentiation and they form more durable memories of brands in consumers' minds.[133]

FIGURE 9.1: % OF IPA DATABANK CASES REPORTING VERY LARGE PROFIT GROWTH (BY COMMUNICATIONS MODEL)

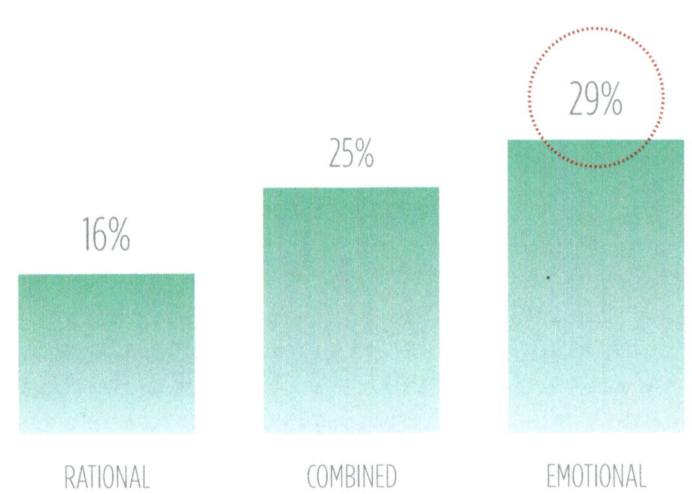

[132] Binet and Field, *Marketing in the Era of Accountability*, pg 12.
[133] Ibid.

Differentiation is a key point; according to the *BrandZ* study, conducted by Kantar Millward Brown, brands that consumers view as different achieve higher value. Those brands that have remained in the top half of the *BrandZ* ranking over the ten years to 2015 were scored highly on 'difference' by consumers, and grew 124% in brand value. In contrast, brands in the bottom half of the ranking scored lower and have increased by only 24% in value.[134]

The effects of emotional campaigns also last much longer than rational campaigns and they tend to accumulate more strongly over time. This is especially true of profitability (see Figure 9.2).[135]

FIGURE 9.2: % OF IPA DATABANK CASES REPORTING VERY LARGE PROFIT GROWTH (BY CAMPAIGN DURATION)

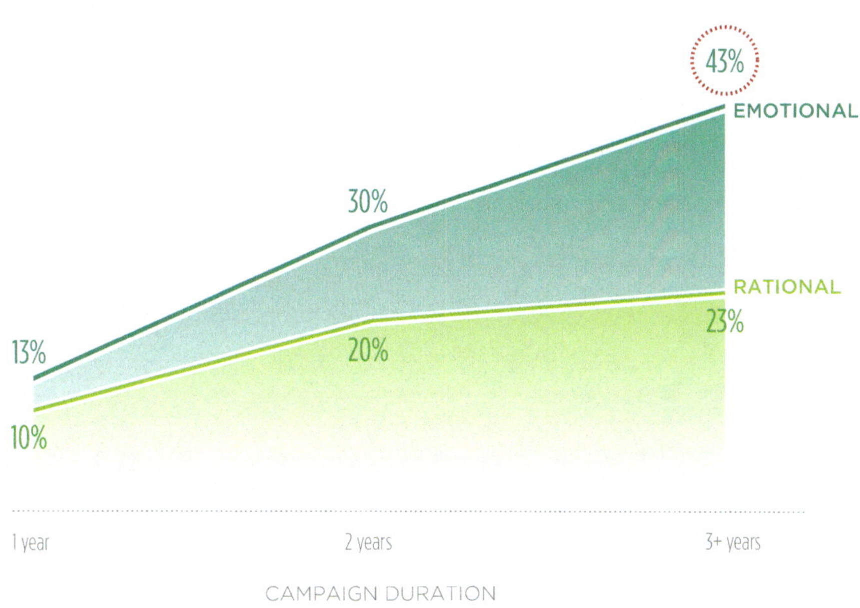

[134] Kantar Millward Brown. *BrandZ™ Top 100 Most Valuable Global Brands (10th Anniversary Edition)*. 2015.
[135] Binet and Field, *The Long and the Short of It*, pg 69.

Based on this evidence, it is no surprise that the percentage of campaigns (in the IPA Databank) using emotional creative strategies is increasing (see Figure 9.3), particularly for creatively-awarded campaigns.[136]

FIGURE 9.3: % OF IPA DATABANK CASES USING EMOTIONAL CREATIVE STRATEGIES

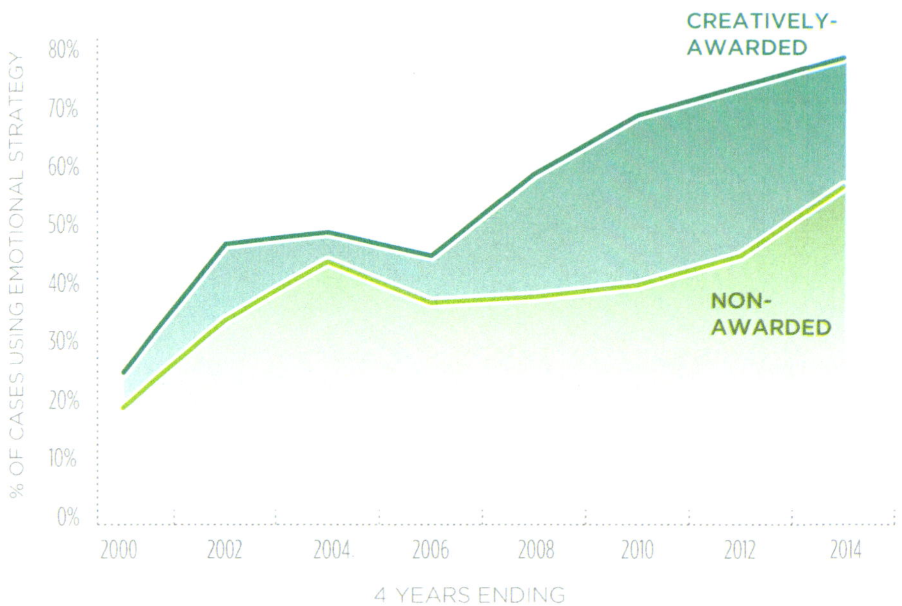

Brand favourability correlates with the emotional content of advertisements, not the 'persuasive' information in them

136 Field, *Selling Creativity Short*, pg 11.

Binet and Field's findings are consistent with a large volume of historic research carried out into the role that emotion plays in the processing of communications. Robert Heath and Paul Feldwick undertook a comprehensive review of this body of evidence for a paper presented at the fiftieth UK Market Research Society Conference in 2007. Heath and Feldwick were certainly rigorous, citing seventy-three different references in their analysis. They were very critical of traditional information-processing models of how advertising works and demonstrated how psychology and neuroscience provide far more convincing explanations. They concluded that *'all decision-making is founded in the emotions'*.[137]

Further validation can be found in more recent work by Robert Heath (2014), which showed that increases in brand favourability correlated with the *emotional* content of advertisements, not the *persuasive information* in them.[138]

Emotionally-based campaigns outperform rationally-based campaigns on every business measure over the long term

Rational campaigns do enjoy an advantage in relation to short-term direct effects, but this advantage is temporary

137 Heath, Robert and Feldwick, Paul. *50 Years Using the Wrong Model of TV Advertising*. International Journal of Market Research, 50(1). 2008.

138 Heath, Robert. *TV Strategy: The Art of Subconscious Seduction*. Admap. 2014.

We will now return to the issue raised at the start of this chapter. Emotional campaigns significantly outperform rational campaigns after a period of six months, but rational campaigns are more effective at directly influencing consumer behaviour in the short-term e.g., calling a phone number, visiting a website or trialling a new product (see Figure 9.4).

This is because rational messaging tends only to strongly influence people who are close to the moment of purchase, whereas people who are not actively engaged in purchasing tend to screen out rational product messages, but emotional influences are much less likely to be filtered.[139]

FIGURE 9.4: % OF IPA DATABANK CASES REPORTING VERY LARGE DIRECT EFFECTS (BY COMMUNICATIONS MODEL)

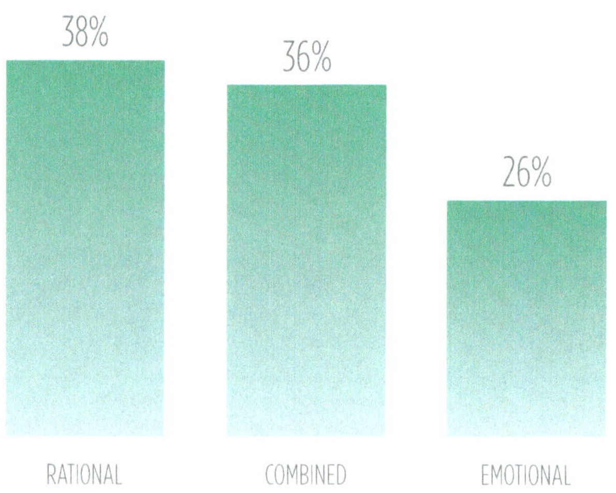

139 Binet and Field, *The Long and the Short of It*, pg 69.

However, this is not a question of 'either or'; both have a role to play in marketing communications and marketers should devise their strategies adopting a balanced approach, which drives long-term brand preference through emotion and short-term sales through rational messaging. The chart below (see Figure 9.5) shows why this is essential by demonstrating how rational and emotional approaches complement each other over time.

FIGURE 9.5: HOW EFFECTS FROM MULTIPLE EXPOSURES BUILD

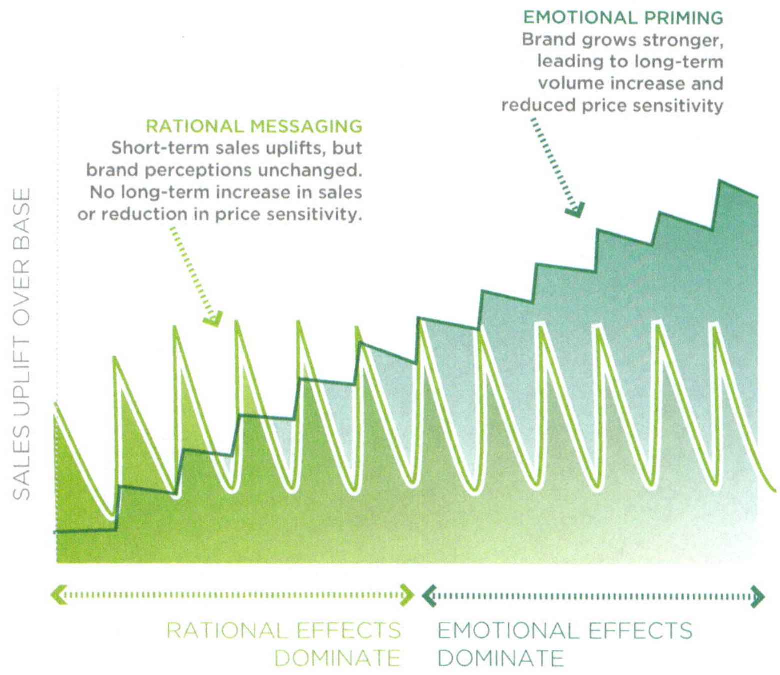

One final point to remember: in addition to apportioning a brand's budget correctly between emotional and rational messages, it is crucial that the correct media channels are used for each approach. Marketers must challenge their agencies on this point. All too often we see campaigns 'shoehorned' into media channels that are ill-equipped to convey the message in the way the creative team intended. Media channels should not just be chosen for the audience they reach, but for their compatibility with the creative strategy employed.

EMOTION AND GREAT PLANNING

A CASE STUDY

CASE STUDY

JOHN LEWIS

Founded in 1864, John Lewis is a UK department store selling fashion, homeware, furniture, sports and electrical items.

In 2009, the company was not trading well; the UK was in a financial crisis and revenue was falling. Like-for-like sales were down 3.4% for the financial year ending January 2009 and operating profit had dropped by 26%.[140] The brand was suffering from low frequency of purchase and low share-of-wallet among its key customers.

It turned to marketing for the solution. Following a fundamental review of its strategy, the company decided on a communications approach that would engage with people on an emotional level, to transform indifference towards the brand and attract new higher-spending customers. Emotion is a powerful tool in marketing. Binet and Field concluded in their report *Marketing in the Era of Accountability* that communications models using emotional appeal are more likely to achieve better business results than rationally-based models using information and persuasion.[141] See Chapter 9 for more information on this topic.

Christmas is a critical trading period for John Lewis; the four weeks preceding December 25th typically deliver circa 20% of annual sales and 40% of annual profit.[142] Therefore, the festive period was used as the springboard and focal point for the company's new communications strategy. Rather than follow the conventional approach for Christmas retail advertising, John Lewis positioned itself as the home of thoughtful gifting, celebrating those who put more care into selecting and giving a gift. The Christmas 2009 commercial *Remember the Feeling* (Figure 9.6) showed children playing with adult gifts and morphing into grown-ups, with the intention of reminding

140 Golding, David et al. *John Lewis: Making the Nation Cry... and Buy.* Warc. 2012.
141 Binet and Field, *Marketing in the Era of Accountability*, pg 12.
142 Golding, David et al., *John Lewis.*

people of the *'magic and fevered excitement'* of Christmas. It used a well-known emotionally-moving track re-recorded by a contemporary artist, a model which it has consistently used ever since. This campaign launched one of the most effective long-term marketing strategies ever seen, and its Christmas campaigns have been the bedrock of its strategy.

John Lewis uses econometric modelling to determine what is driving its revenue. In addition to isolating the impact of marketing, it helps the company to understand the effects of many other variables including weather and pricing. The modelling has proven that the company's investment in advertising generated over £1.75 billion in extra sales revenue during the first five years (from 2009 to 2013), and over £450 million in additional profit. That's more than £5 extra profit for every £1 spent on advertising.[143]

FIGURE 9.6: IMAGES FROM *REMEMBER THE FEELING* TV COMMERCIAL

143 adam&eveDDB London. *John Lewis: Monty's Christmas.* Warc. 2016.

The Christmas campaigns, in particular, have proven to be the most effective, increasing sales by an average of 16%[144] (Figure 9.7). They also drive the most profit; for example, John Lewis' 2014 Christmas campaign generated a net profit of £32.4m, or £7.39 for every £1 invested in advertising[145] - an astonishing result (Figure 9.8).

FIGURE 9.7: CONTRIBUTION OF ADVERTISING TO JOHN LEWIS SALES

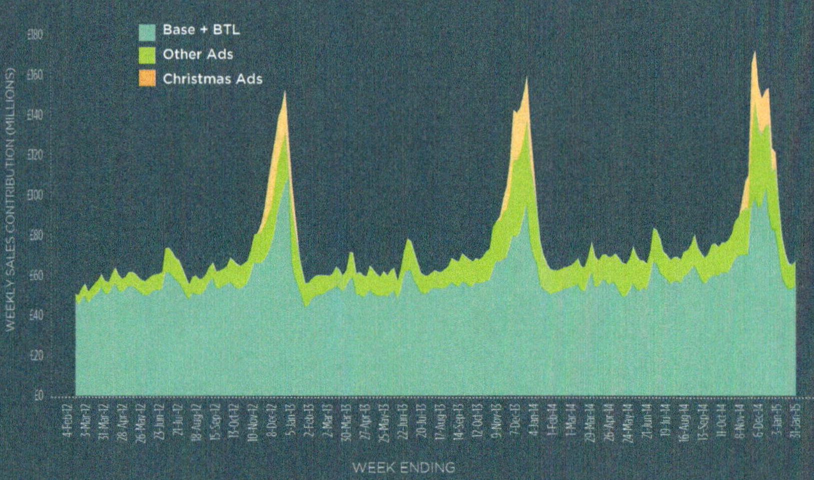

FIGURE 9.8: ECONOMETRICS: RETURN ON INVESTMENT ANALYSIS CHRISTMAS 2014

John Lewis ad spend	£4.4m
Incremental revenue generated (incl VAT)	£132.8m
Revenue generated per £1 spent	£30.29m
Net profit (after deducting ad spend)	£32.4m
Net profit per £1 spent	£7.39
Return on marketing investment	739%

[144] Binet, Les et al. *The Gift That Keeps on Giving: John Lewis Christmas Advertising, 2012-2015*. Warc. 2016.
[145] Ibid.

But it wasn't just down to the creative platform, John Lewis took the long-term view, didn't waver from its strategy and invested consistently. In addition, the emotional creative ensured that the communications were shared between people, talked about in the media, ultimately entering popular culture. It is also interesting to note that the company followed best practice in striking the right balance between long-term and short-term marketing investment; by 2015, its Christmas budget was split almost exactly 60:40 between brand work and supplier-funded activation,[146] in line with Binet and Field's conclusions covered in Chapter 8 of this book.

Perhaps the most striking proof of the success of this sustained and consistent marketing strategy is the growth in market share that John Lewis has achieved. Since launching the strategy in 2009, the company's market share has increased from 22.8% to 29.6% in 2015.[147] This is an extraordinary result in a mature, highly competitive sector.

FIGURE 9.9: JOHN LEWIS MARKET SHARE

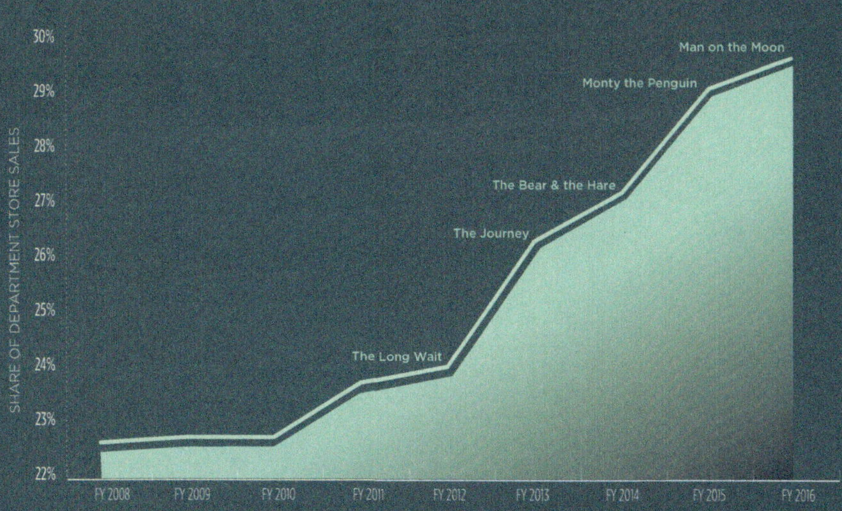

Agencies: adam&eveDDB and Manning Gottlieb OMD

146 Binet, *The Gift That Keeps on Giving*, pg 132.
147 Ibid.

CHAPTER 10

PENETRATION VS LOYALTY

Despite convincing and verified evidence that recruiting new customers is more profitable than trying to increase frequency of purchase, the debate of penetration versus loyalty still rages on. While debate is a healthy thing, it needs to be evidence-based and, thankfully, in this case there is a wealth of reputable and robust research from well-respected practitioners, such as Andrew Ehrenberg, Byron Sharp, Les Binet and Peter Field to illuminate the subject.

Although marketing is both an art and a science, there has been too little of the latter applied to the choices that are made in the industry, and as Bryon Sharp remarked in an Admap article in 2010, *'Like any other profession (e.g., engineering, medicine), marketers who understand fundamental scientific laws are vastly better at their job.'*[148]

Double Jeopardy is a long-standing empirical marketing law that shows (with few exceptions) that penetration and purchase frequency are inextricably linked; bigger brands have more customers who buy slightly more often, and brands with small market shares have fewer buyers and lower brand loyalty. This law applies across categories ranging from laundry detergent to aviation fuel[149] and across countries and time.[150]

The implication of this law is that a marketer should focus on penetration to grow sales. If the brand's customer base increases, then brand loyalty will also increase as a consequence.

148 Sharp, Byron and Newstead, Kate. *Loyalty is not the Holy Grail.* Admap. 2010.

149 Ehrenberg, Andrew S. C.; Goodhardt, Gerald G.; and Barwise, Patrick. *Double Jeopardy Revisited.* Journal of Marketing. 54(3). 1990.

150 Ehrenberg, Andrew S. C.; Uncles, Mark D.; and Goodhardt, Gerald G. *Understanding Brand Performance Measures: Using Dirichlet Benchmarks.* Journal of Business Research. 57(12). 2004.

One of the great authorities on this subject was the late statistician Andrew Ehrenberg, who popularised the *Double Jeopardy* law and carried out extensive analyses of consumer purchase data over many years. His research proposed that loyalty is not a key determinant of success and that penetration has a much bigger impact on market share. He wrote in 1974:

'In general, there are relatively few 100% loyal or sole buyers of a brand, especially over any extended period of time. A typical and predictable finding for frequently bought grocery products is that in a week, 80 or 90% of buyers of a brand buy only that brand, that in half a year the proportion is down to 30%, and that in a year, only 10% of buyers are 100% loyal. To expect any substantial group or segment of consumers to be uniquely attracted to one particular selling proposition or advertising platform would therefore generally seem entirely beside the point.'[151]

While some people had criticised Ehrenberg's work for being focused on FMCG brands, Binet and Field were later able to prove that Ehrenberg's law consistently holds true regardless of the category analysed.[152]

Binet and Field first wrote about the subject in 2007. Their analysis of the IPA databank of case studies showed that loyalty-based marketing only rarely leads to successful marketing outcomes and that only 9% of loyalty campaigns actually increase loyalty significantly. Their work, like that of Ehrenberg, suggested that when marketing works, the payback mostly comes from the 'long tail' of non-users and light users.[153]

They wrote, *'This does not mean that loyalty is irrelevant, or that firms should ignore their existing customers in favour of new ones. Some marketing that attempts to build loyalty does turn out to be highly profitable. But the databank suggests that when such loyalty campaigns do work, they do so mainly by recruiting new customers, not by reducing churn or by extracting more value from existing ones.'*[154]

[151] Ehrenberg, Andrew S. C. *Repetitive Advertising and the Consumer*. Journal of Advertising Research, 40(6), 2000. (1974 article re-published)
[152] Binet and Field, *Marketing in the Era of Accountability*, pg 12.
[153] Ibid.
[154] Ibid.

In a later study *Selling Creativity Short* (2016), Field expanded on this point, *'Loyalty strategies,'* he wrote, *'can produce cost-effective short-term activation effects, but the true cost of this is long-term ineffectiveness.'*[155]

Yet many practitioners still believe that loyalty-based marketing is a more profitable endeavour than growing the penetration of their brands. It is true that loyalty schemes have a place in the marketing mix, although when it comes to long-term brand growth, the evidence clearly shows that penetration almost always wins.

Generally speaking, loyalty schemes do not create loyalty; they tend to cement already existing loyalty.[156] Marketers must ask themselves if the money invested in these programmes would deliver more sales overall if it was invested in driving penetration instead.

Marketers should advertise to everyone in the market for their product, rather than focusing on a small segmented audience

In 2010, Byron Sharp made quite an impact on the marketing industry with his book *How Brands Grow*. Based on extensive research and mathematics, he also found that loyalty programmes have little effect, and that marketers should advertise to everyone in the market for their product, rather than focusing on a small segmented audience. In his view, the potential gains from customer acquisition dwarf the potential gains from retention.[157]

155 Field, *Selling Creativity Short*, pg 11.
156 Warc. *What We Know About Brand Loyalty*. Warc Best Practice. October 2016.
157 Sharp, Byron. *How Brands Grow: What Marketers Don't Know*. Oxford University Press. 2010.

'Penetration,' he wrote, *'comes from extending a brand's mental and physical availability, making it easier to buy for more people...To grow brand share, you need a lot more light buyers and a few more heavy buyers. Strategies that concentrate only on heavy customers will not turn a small brand into a big one.'*[158]

Sharp did not pull any punches; he wrote, *'Knowledge of scientific laws can lead to insight, prediction and understanding. If all brand managers had known of these laws, billions of dollars would not have been spent on poor performing marketing investments like loyalty programmes.'*[159]

Of course, some people disagree; Oliver Hupp of GFK Germany published an article in Admap (September 2016)[160] which contradicts Sharp's work, in particular. Hupp claims that findings from two GFK studies show that *'penetration is not the predominant driver of brand growth and that relationship equity explains the difference in market success.'*

> Penetration is three times more likely to be the main driver of growth and profit compared with loyalty

Although not directed at anyone in particular, Sharp wrote a blog (also in September 2016) entitled *Answering Critics.*[161] It was a stinging rebuke and well worth reading. He finished by saying *'Please put the data in the public domain, or at least show the world some easy-to-understand tables of data. If you want us to consider your claims seriously then please don't hide behind obscure statistics and jargon.'*

158 Sharp and Newstead, *Loyalty is not the Holy Grail*, pg 135.
159 Sharp, *How Brands Grow*, pg 137.
160 Hupp, Oliver. *Loyalty is the Key Driver of Brand Growth*. Admap. September 2016.
161 Sharp, Byron. *Marketing Science Commentary*. September 2016.

Recently, in November 2016, Binet and Field returned to the loyalty vs. penetration topic at *Effectiveness Week* in London. Field put it clearly: *'If you are tightly targeted at known consumers then you don't generate long-term profit growth'.*[162] They shared some new empirical data showing that penetration is three times more likely to be the main driver of growth and profit compared with loyalty (see Figure 10.1). Their analysis showed that very large business effects were seen in 7% of loyalty-only campaigns, whereas this increased to 22% of penetration-only campaigns.[163]

FIGURE 10.1: % OF IPA DATABANK CASES REPORTING VERY LARGE BUSINESS EFFECTS (LOYALTY VS. PENETRATION)

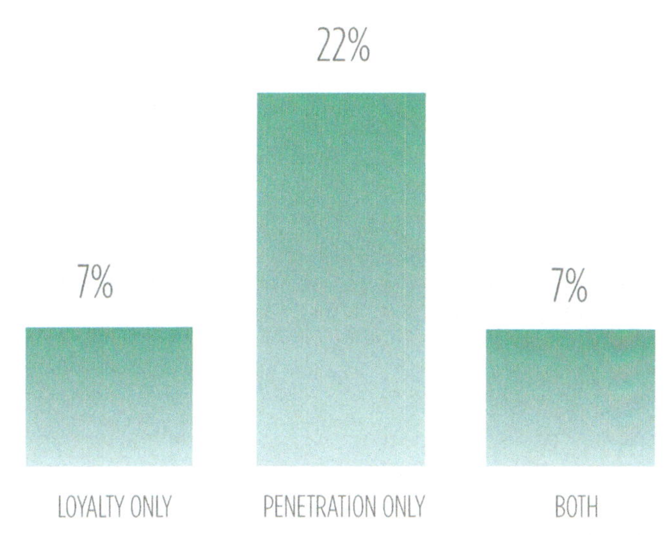

Binet and Field amplified the argument further, by demonstrating that mass marketing is still a driver of growth. They shared some data on how campaign reach is more effective in growing market share.

162 Binet and Field, *Marketing in the Digital Age*, pg 13.
163 Ibid.

Figure 10.2 shows that campaigns targeting existing customers only grew market share by 1.2%, campaigns targeting non-customers only grew by 1.4%, but mass marketing campaigns targeting both groups grew market share by 1.8%. As Les Binet said at the presentation, *'There is no sign in the data that mass marketing is becoming less effective'*[164]. The tools are changing, but the rules are not.

FIGURE 10.2: ANNUAL MARKET SHARE GROWTH ACHIEVED (TARGETING CUSTOMERS VS. NON-CUSTOMERS)

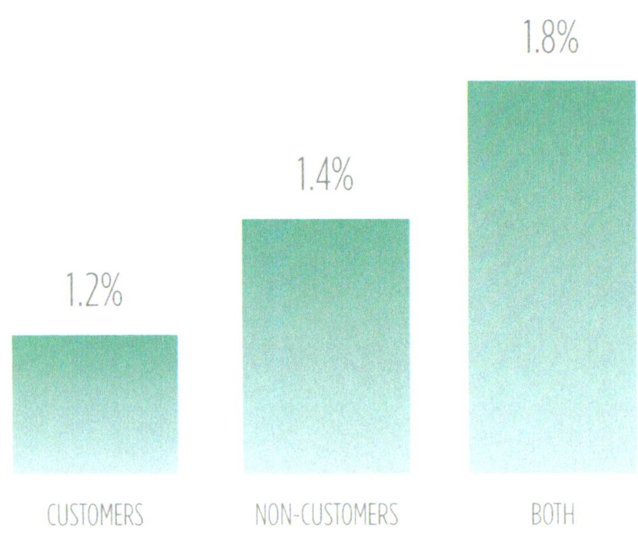

Despite the relentless pace of technology, the fragmentation of media and our increased ability to target our audiences more tightly, one truth still remains, the most successful consumer brands in the world will be the ones that appeal to a large base of people. Rather than use technology to exclude people, we should use it to facilitate placing more relevant messages in front of them.

164 Binet and Field, *Marketing in the Digital Age*, pg 13.

This quote from ad-contrarian Bob Hoffman, sums it up nicely:

'The people who keep insisting that mass media and mass marketing are dead are brilliant at seeing all the trees, but are blind to the forest. They know about every app, every widget, and every website, but they can't see that it's all melding with TV, print, direct mail, outdoor and radio to create an even more pervasive mega-medium that is affecting everything we say and do.'[165]

[165] Hoffman, Bob. *The Mass Marketing Zombie*. The Ad Contrarian. February 2012.

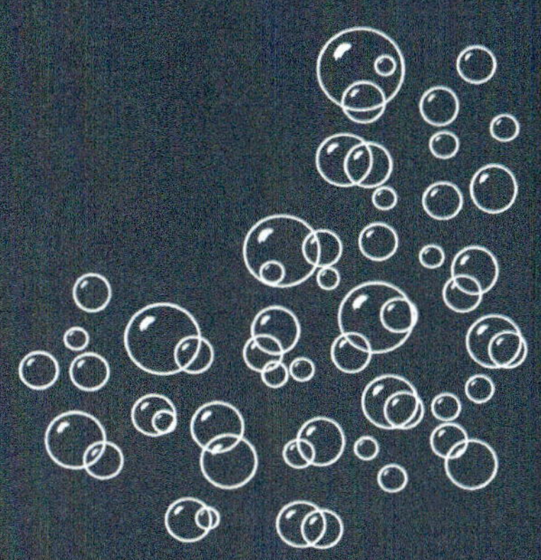

PENETRATION THROUGH CREATIVITY

TWO CASE STUDIES

CASE STUDY

COCA-COLA

The Coca-Cola Company's brands are consumed more than 1.9 billion times every day.[166] Coca-Cola is the fourth most valuable brand in the world, worth $58.5 billion.[167] Its trademark is recognised by 94% of the earth's population.[168] The company understands the vital role that advertising has played in its success and continues to invest large sums every year, spending $3.3 billion in 2013, $3.5 billion in 2014 and $4.0 billion in 2015 to promote its portfolio of soft drinks brands, which includes fourteen brands that generate more than $1 billion in retail sales value.[169] Its advertising investment in 2015 accounted for 9% of global net operating revenues.[170] The Coca-Cola Company has stated that its commitment to advertising reflects the need to strengthen its brands. It realises the importance of this investment now, more than ever, as it invests more in marketing its lower and no sugar brands, such as Coca-Cola Zero Sugar in the UK, and in launching new brands in response to changing consumer trends.

At the time of writing, despite very challenging times, The Coca-Cola Company ranks as the most effective marketer in the world, and brand Coke is the world's most effective brand, according to New York-based Effie global effectiveness index 2016.

FIGURE 10.3 : COCA-COLA'S FIRST AD FEATURING HADDON SUNDBLOM'S DEPICTION OF SANTA IN 1931.

166 The Coca-Cola Company. *Annual Report (Form 10K)*. US: The Coca-Cola Company. 2015.
167 Forbes. *The World's Most Valuable Brands*. 2017.
168 The Coca-Cola Company. *Who We Are*. Infograph. 2017.
169 The Coca-Cola Company, *Annual Report*.
170 Ibid.

Of course, it's not just about spending money on placing advertising in the media to drive penetration, there must be a great creative idea at the heart of the campaign to maximise the effect. Let's look at two examples of great marketing from the company: the *Magic Bow* and *Share a Coke* campaigns.

MAGIC BOW CAMPAIGN

Coca-Cola has a long association with Christmas and bringing families together during the holidays. In fact, the modern image of Santa Claus was created for Coca-Cola marketing campaigns. Although Santa was depicted in a red costume before becoming a 'brand ambassador' for Coke, he was illustrated in many different ways. The modern image that we all associate with Santa Claus was commissioned by The Coca-Cola Company and developed by Michigan-born illustrator Haddon Sundblom (see Figure 10.3), who continued to paint Santa Claus for Coca-Cola's Christmas campaigns every year from 1931 to 1964.

Christmas continues to play a key role in Coca-Cola's marketing to the present day. The following is an example of a creative idea that was developed in Columbia in 2013 and subsequently launched in many countries

FIGURE 10.4 THE MAGIC BOW

Almost 140 million Magic Bow bottles were sold in Europe alone around the world.

The idea was to turn the Coca-Cola bottle into a gift by creating an innovative label that could be transformed into a bow by pulling a strip. Simple but very effective. It was then amplified through advertising and other forms of marketing communication.

The campaign had a strong impact in each market it was deployed in. In 2015, the markets that ran with *Magic Bow* saw a volume sales increase of 13.1% in November and 7.8% in December versus the same months in 2014, compared with an average increase of 6.7% and 3.8% respectively in countries that didn't use *Magic Bow*. Almost 140 million *Magic Bow* bottles were sold in Europe alone.[171]

SHARE A COKE

In this example, we see the power of another simple idea; The Coca-Cola Company printed people's names on bottles and cans to encourage the public to buy personalised product packs for themselves and for friends and family. The idea was first launched in Australia in 2011, using 150 of the most popular names in the country. It was a commercial success, increasing consumption among the core target of young adults by 7%. It also succeeded in getting 5% of Australians to drink Coke for the first time, or for the first time in over a year.[172] Since then,

FIGURE 10.5: THE SHARE A COKE CAMPAIGN

[171] Ogilvy & Mather Bogotá. *Coca-Cola: The Gift Bottle*. Warc. 2016.
[172] Cyron, Gerald. *Coca-Cola: Share a Coke (Australia)*. Warc. 2012.

this initiative has been used in circa eighty countries.

The campaign's first outing in the US was in the summer of 2014 and turned out to be one of the best-performing marketing initiatives in the company's history. The backdrop was not positive - the carbonated soft drinks market was (and continues to be) highly challenged as consumers increasingly seek healthier alternatives such as juices, flavoured waters and smoothies. This trend resulted in a decline in US market sales of 3.3% in 2013.

So, the US business imported the Share a Coke concept and 'upped the ante' on the Australian campaign by printing 250 of the most common American names on its twenty-ounce bottles. The results outperformed expectations; 1.25 million more Americans tried a Coke and sales of participating packages rose by 11%.

The campaign also contributed to stemming the sales decline for The Coca-Cola Company's US business as a whole, with volumes rising by 0.4% and revenue increasing by 2.5% during the active period – a remarkable result after eleven consecutive years of sales decline.[173] The company also achieved a 2% unit price increase amidst competitor discounting.[174]

Due to this success, *Share a Coke* ran again in 2015, this time with 1,000 names – four times the number of 2014.

1.25 million more Americans tried a Coke and sales of participating packages rose by 11%

Agencies: Ogilvy Bogotá (Magic Bow). Ogilvy Sydney, Starcom Mediavest Group US and Wieden & Kennedy US (Share a Coke).

173 Mendoza, Luis. *Coca-Cola: Share a Coke (US)*. Warc. 2015.
174 Esterel, Mike. *'Share a Coke' Credited With a Pop in Sales*. The Wall Street Journal. 2014.

CHAPTER 11

CREATIVITY MATTERS: IT DELIVERS STRONGER BUSINESS EFFECTS

There tends to be a large amount of cynicism in marketing circles regarding the purpose of creative awards. The issue is probably summed up best by comments from Donald Gunn, included in James Hurman's excellent book, *The Case for Creativity:*

'In our business there is a substantial body of opinion that is dismissive, if not scornful, about creative awards. These industry colleagues - and they exist both at clients and in agencies - take the view that awards are basically a frivolity, and are wholly irrelevant, indeed probably counterproductive, to the main business in hand - the selling of products and services.'[175]

The truth is that creativity has a profound and quantifiable influence on marketing effectiveness. There are a number of studies that support this; research carried out in Ireland by Hand and McGrath found compelling evidence of a creativity dividend. They noted that creatively-awarded campaigns are more efficient than non-awarded campaigns by around ten times.[176]

Creativity has a profound and quantifiable influence on marketing effectiveness

175 Hurman, James. *The Case for Creativity*. New Zealand: AUT Media. 2011.

176 Hand and McGrath, *A Line in the Sand*, pg 71.

The most compelling and robust analysis was conducted by Peter Field for the IPA (UK) in 2010,[177] 2011[178] and 2016.[179] In total, Field scrutinised a twenty-year dataset of 479 case studies to quantify the impact of creativity on marketing. In his latest report *Selling Creativity Short* (2016), Field states that creatively-awarded campaigns achieve six times the efficiency of non-awarded campaigns.[180] In fact, the more awarded the creative work, the more effective it was.

Creatively-awarded campaigns achieve six times the efficiency of non-awarded campaigns

By efficiency, Field is referring to the relationship between a brand's growth in market share and its share of category communications expenditure (*share of voice*). In particular, Field homes in on *extra share of voice* (ESOV), which is the brand's *share of voice* minus its *share of market*. Research by Binet, Field and others, such as John Philip Jones, has established that there is a strong relationship between ESOV and market share growth.

A multiple of six is impressive, but in Field's previous report in 2011 (which covers campaigns prior to the global financial crisis), it was a staggering 12.4.[181] During the recession years that followed, there has been a significant move towards short-termism in marketing (explained in Chapter 8), coupled with a decline in marketing communications investment levels. These factors, Field claims, have been directly responsible for halving the effectiveness of creativity (in advertising) during the decade to 2014.

Between 2006 and 2014 average budgets (expressed as ESOV), for campaigns in the IPA Databank, have fallen by twelve percentage points. However, for creatively-awarded campaigns the decline has been twenty percentage points, taking them into negative ESOV territory for the first time in the twenty-year run of data.[182]

177 Field, *The Link Between Creativity and Effectiveness*, pg 70.
178 Field, Peter. *The Link Between Creativity and Effectiveness (Update)*. UK: Institute of Practitioners in Advertising (IPA). 2011.
179 Field, *Selling Creativity Short*, pg 11.
180 Ibid.
181 Field, *The Link Between Creativity and Effectiveness (Update)*.
182 Field, *Selling Creativity Short*.

Marketers seem to be hoping that the creativity of campaigns will be a substitute for putting budget behind them in media, but as Field states in his report, growth is generally not achieved unless effective advertising is combined with a level of investment that is above maintenance weight.

The importance of effective advertising is also quantified in the *BrandZ* study, conducted by Kantar Millward Brown; it found that brands that combined a strong brand proposition with excellent advertising, achieved value growth of 168% over the ten-year period between 2006 and 2015. Those brands with just a strong proposition only grew by half that rate, at 76%.[183]

Although the global financial crisis has dissipated, there is no sign of best practice returning. The habits of the recession years seem to be holding firm. This represents an opportunity for businesses to take heed and use the multiplier effect of creativity, combined with optimal investment levels, to drive real growth.

This quote from Peter Field is a good way to round off the argument:

'Marketers need a balanced long, mid and short-term investment strategy if they are to optimise value creation and return on marketing investment (ROMI). They also need a commitment to creativity. Creativity is not just a rescue strategy for an underinvested brand. It is the cornerstone for sound business management.'[184]

183 Kantar Millward Brown. *BrandZ™ Top 100 Most Valuable Global Brands*, pg 123.
184 Field, *Selling Creativity Short*, pg 11.

CREATIVITY TRUMPS EVERYTHING

A CASE STUDY

CASE STUDY

VOLVO

This case study is a strong example of how to make 'earned media' work for a business-to-business (B2B) brand. Earned media describes the 'free' publicity that a brand achieves through online sharing, editorial coverage, product reviews, blog mentions, social media posts and other forms of online dialogue.

Volvo Group is a truck business based in Sweden, serving a relatively small global market, with annual sales of 207,475 units (2015) across six brands - Volvo, UD, Renault, Mack, Eicher and Dongfeng.[185]

In 2012/13 the company launched a new line of Volvo-branded heavy-duty trucks in Europe, with a marketing programme that featured specific technical aspects of each vehicle. In the past, products like these were promoted using typical B2B marketing practices - long on detail and short on creativity. The small size of B2B markets usually restricts marketing communications to trade media, search marketing or direct channels. This can often constrain creative thinking, but not in Volvo's case; they broke the mould with this highly imaginative campaign.

The products certainly deserved a televisual canvas to communicate the importance of the new innovations, but the market for trucks is too small for a brand to promote itself on large-scale media formats, particularly TV. The wastage would be unacceptably high.

Volvo's creative agency, Forsman & Bodenfors, devised a solution that achieved the televisual impact required, without spending millions on TV. They could afford to produce big commercial assets with high production values, but not to broadcast them through paid media.

[185] Volvo Group. *The Volvo Group Annual and Sustainability Report.* 2015.

However, if they could make commercials that the target market really wanted to see and share, then they could use direct channels/owned media to hit their key audience and social media/PR to broaden the reach. This would mean going beyond truck fleet buyers to other key influencers, who have a say; i.e., the drivers, their families and friends.

Of course, this is far easier said than done. In fact, viral campaigns like this rarely succeed, because very few creative concepts/executions are special enough. It would not be a viable or recommended strategy in most situations, but in a tightly defined segment like this one, the risk was lower because it was possible to share the commercials with the core target through direct channels. Also, the agency and the client knew they had a superior campaign idea.

Forsman & Bodenfors developed a series of six cinematic-style 'live test' videos to promote specific technical features of each truck in powerful and unexpected ways. The series featured stunts performed by a ballerina, a hamster and the president of Volvo Trucks, but the most successful commercial was for the FM truck, which focussed in on its innovative Dynamic Steering feature.

The one-minute video, entitled *The Epic Split*, featured the famous martial arts action movie star, Jean-Claude Van Damme, performing a spectacular stunt with two Volvo FM trucks.

Shot in a single take, at dawn on an airstrip in Spain, Van Damme performed his famous 'splits' stunt, standing on the wing mirrors of two trucks, while they were reversing at low speed – an extraordinary demonstration of the precision of Volvo Dynamic Steering, which enabled two truck drivers to maintain the exact same distance apart. This video became the biggest hit of the series, collecting eighty-five million views (at the time of writing) and 20,000 editorial reports in the media worldwide.[186]

[186] The Best of Global Digital Marketing. *Case Study: Volvo Trucks Live Test Series.* 2016.

FIGURE 11.1: JEAN-CLAUDE VAN DAMME PERFORMING HIS *EPIC SPLIT* ON TWO VOLVO FM TRUCKS

It is estimated that the whole campaign of six videos achieved €126 million worth of earned media.[187] Brand consideration among truck buyers, as measured through research, increased by 46%,[188] and according to Olof Persson, President and CEO of Volvo Group, the campaign contributed to a *'historically high'* increase in market share in Europe. Most importantly, sales in the fourth quarter of 2013 (immediately after the campaign period) increased by 24%.[189]

Sales in the fourth quarter of 2013 (immediately after the campaign period) increased by 24%

[187] The Best of Global Digital Marketing, *Case Study*, pg 155.
[188] Iyer, Byravee. *Volvo Insiders on Creating, and Following up on, the 'Epic Split'*. Campaign Asia. September 2014.
[189] Forsman & Bodenfors. *Volvo Trucks: Live Test Series*. Warc. 2015.

The campaign also had another benefit - it boosted internal pride / confidence in the organisation and it gave the Volvo Trucks sales people a new conversation starter. This knock-on morale benefit is often overlooked in marketing. The innovative nature of the work also produced a positive 'halo effect' on the Volvo brand in general, across all its forms.

It's important to point out that examples like this are the exception that break the rule. Planning a campaign that relies on earned media alone in a tight small B2B market segment is risky, but aiming to do it in a large consumer market segment would be foolhardy. As covered in the next chapter of this book, there is clear evidence that earned and owned media are effective, but not on their own. As Les Binet said at *Effectiveness Week* in London (2016), *'Having viral success without any budget, and generating significant profit for brands, very, very rarely happens. Earned media is a consequence of paid media, by and large.'*[190]

The campaign of six videos achieved €126 million worth of earned media

---

Agency: Forsman & Bodenfors

[190] Clift, *Marketing in the Digital Age*, pg 110.

CHAPTER 12

THE VALUE OF OWNED & EARNED MEDIA

While the level of investment in buying advertising space is crucial in most marketing campaigns, there are times when the investment in creative has a disproportionate impact that can be augmented through owned and earned media. Although they cannot be relied upon as consistently as paid media, they are a valuable parts of the marketing mix.

Earned media, in particular, can be enormously effective if the creative work lights a spark with consumers and becomes viral. In addition to spreading the word farther, it can be effective in driving demand for the product due to the trust people have in word-of-mouth forms of communication. Content delivered in this environment contributes to building credibility for brands.

Earned media covers the 'free' publicity that a brand achieves through online sharing, editorial coverage, product reviews, blog mentions, social media posts and other forms of online dialogue. Owned media are the channels controlled by a brand, such as a website, Twitter account, Facebook page, blog or email.

Nielsen conducted a global study into advertising trust in 2015 and earned media came out on top. The chart overleaf shows the percent of global respondents who completely or somewhat trust earned and owned formats.[191]

[191] Nielsen. *Global Trust in Advertising: Winning Strategies for an Evolving Media Landscape*. 2015.

FIGURE 12.1: NIELSEN GLOBAL STUDY INTO ADVERTISING TRUST

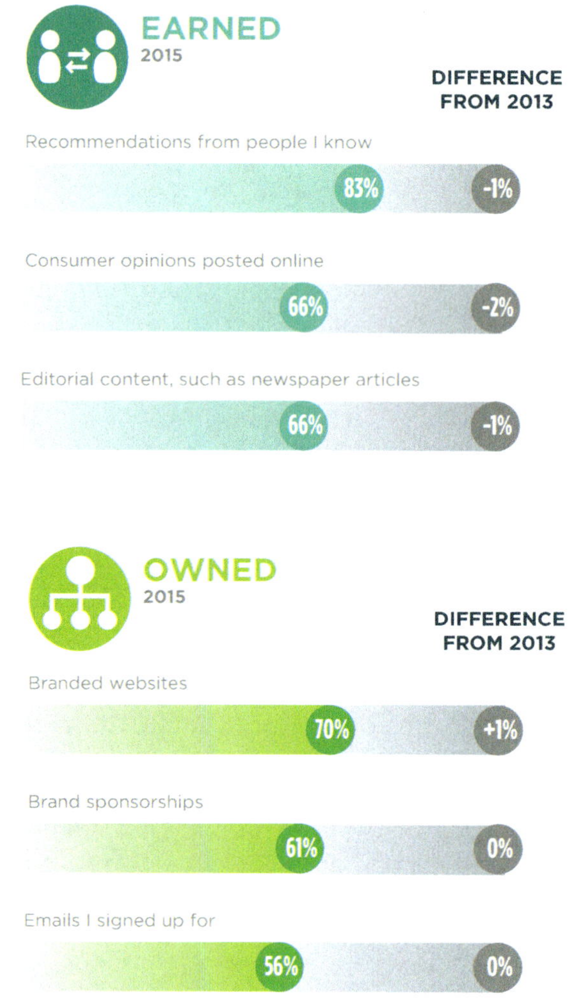

Brands using paid media typically grow three times faster than those that just rely on owned and earned media

However, as mentioned earlier, the extent of earned media that a brand secures in a campaign cannot be predicted in advance. It takes a very special piece of content marketing to catch the imagination of people. Also, it rarely works alone; therefore, it is important to create a complete strategy that optimises the use of paid, owned and earned media.

This is borne out in the latest research conducted by Binet and Field for the IPA, released in November 2016; it shows that brands using paid media typically grow three times faster than those that just rely on owned and earned media. However, the report goes on to say that paid media will only be at their most effective when combined with strong earned and owned strands.

> Owned media typically increase the effectiveness of a paid campaign by 13% and earned media by 26%

The research found that adding owned media to a paid campaign typically increases its effectiveness by 13%, while adding earned media causes an increase of 26%.[192] However, Binet and Field go on to say that they found almost no examples of campaigns generating strong effects without having paid media in place.

[192] Clift, *Marketing in the Digital Age*, pg 110.

FORESIGHT, DISTINCTIVENESS AND FLAIR

A CASE STUDY

CASE STUDY

ORCHARD THIEVES

For decades, being a cider drinker in Ireland meant being a Bulmers drinker; the brand had dominated the category for thirty years, with a market share of 80% (2014).[193] A number of new entrants tried to break in over the years, but none succeeded in challenging Bulmers' position.

Bulmers did not achieve 80% share just because of its product credentials; it built and protected its position over many years through consistent, award-winning marketing campaigns. However, in recent years its investment in marketing had been falling, leaving the door slightly open, but it would require another brilliant piece of marketing to seize the opportunity.

FIGURE 12.2: ESTIMATED ADVERTISING SPEND FOR BULMERS IN REPUBLIC OF IRELAND

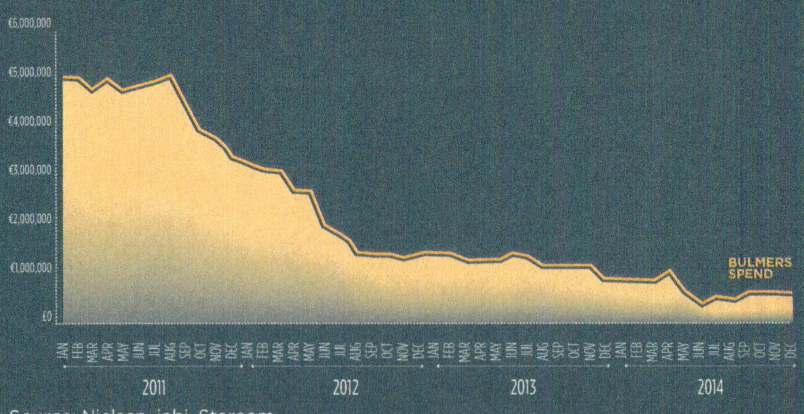

Source: Nielsen, iabi, Starcom

193 Rothco and Starcom Ireland. *Orchard Thieves: Thieving the Spotlight.* Warc. 2016. The source for Bulmers' market share is Nielsen.

The importance of consistent investment cannot be overstated here. The impact of budget cutting is not fully understood in this industry. Research clearly shows the damage caused by inconsistent marketing. Typically, when a brand's budget is cut, it continues to benefit from the momentum of the investment it made in marketing over the previous years. This tends to mitigate any short-term business effects and results in a dangerously misleading increase in short-term profitability.[194] The longer-term business harm is more considerable, but goes unnoticed at first, leaving the brand open to attack.

This type of behaviour often occurs during periods of recession, but research is quite clear on this point: brands emerge from economic slumps in a considerably weaker position if they have been subjected to significant cuts in marketing investment during the downturn.[195] Also, companies that consistently advertise during recessions perform better in the long run.

According to research carried out by McGraw Hill in the US, three years after the 1981 – 1982 recession, sales of companies that were aggressive advertisers had risen by 256% over those who cut back and waited for the downturn to pass.[196]

HEINEKEN Ireland realised that to succeed it would have to disrupt the market with a brand that offered a fresh take on cider; Orchard Thieves was born. The name and the fox emblem were sourced from HEINEKEN New Zealand, but everything else was created from scratch. Due to clever exploitation of the fox, the emblem would prove to be a significant factor in the success of the campaign.

194 IPA. *Advertising in a Downturn: A Report of Key Findings From an IPA Seminar.* UK: Institute of Practitioners in Advertising (IPA). March 2008.
195 Ibid.
196 McGraw-Hill Research. *Laboratory of Advertising Performance Report 5262.* US: McGraw-Hill. 1986.

Breaking into an established category is extremely difficult; to put this in context, Orchard Thieves' target in year one was to secure 2% of the cider market, with an ambitious goal of reaching 10% by year five. The key imperative was to drive large-scale trial to convert cider drinkers to the new brand.[197]

The 'behaviour' of Orchard Thieves would prove to be a crucial factor in successfully differentiating it from Bulmers. The marketing team realised that if the brand behaved like a traditional cider, it would be largely ignored. It had to move away from 'apples and orchards' and offer a more contemporary, urban take on cider instead. The personality of the brand, and resulting behaviour, would be summed up by a simple expression of the creative idea, BE BOLD.

FIGURE 12.3: ORCHARD THIEVES' BRAND MANTRA AND CREATIVE EXPRESSION

In practice, this meant imbuing the brand (through marketing communications) with risk-taking characteristics and a personality that's alert, spontaneous and breaks the rules of convention. The creative work developed and how/where it was placed in the media lived up to this. The fox was more than simply an emblem on the pack, it was woven into the brand story and its interactions with consumers.

[197] Rothco and Starcom Ireland, *Orchard Thieves: Thieving the Spotlight*, pg 164.

In a highly-innovative move, the fox interrupted national TV and online video channels as part of a teaser campaign; it hijacked commercials for Meteor (mobile phone network) and Hailo (taxi app). It also disrupted the evening broadcast 'idents' on channel 3e.

FIGURE 12.4: ORCHARD THIEVES HIJACKED COMMERCIALS FOR METEOR AND HAILO

FIGURE 12.5: ORCHARD THIEVES DISRUPTED THE 'IDENTS' ON TV CHANNEL 3E

Intrigue was created on the streets, with projections and graffiti-branded city walls across Ireland, announcing the arrival of Orchard Thieves and its brand mantra *#BeBold*. Anyone who followed the fox on social media was rewarded with a taste of the new cider, some merchandise and an invitation to a 'secret' launch event.

The brand also made excellent use of owned media. *The Bold Hour* was a good example of this; when the clocks moved forward an hour (in March 2016), Orchard Thieves decided to 'steal' it back for its consumers. A branded *Bold Hour* event was held simultaneously in Dublin, Cork and Galway. Consumers signed up at *denofthieves.ie* or responded to an emailed invitation. Traffic levels on the website doubled and sign-ups to *denofthieves.ie* tripled. On this site, consumers could also *thieve* pints, which allowed Orchard Thieves to be sampled at scale in pubs and off-licences nationally.

FIGURE 12.6: ORCHARD THIEVES CREATES INTRIGUE ON THE STREETS

In addition to the innovative activities described above, the brand invested in a solid, consistent campaign across television, out-of-home formats, digital and social media. Earlier in this book, we demonstrated the important correlation that exists between *share of voice* and market share growth (see Chapter 7).

The Orchard Thieves team understood the importance of this and invested strongly behind the brand to put it on a growth trajectory, achieving 45% *share of voice* within the cider category in the first twelve months.

Orchard Thieves is an exceptional success story. The brand was launched in May 2015 and within six months it achieved 85% awareness and 57% trial. Its market share smashed through the 2% short-term target within weeks; by the end of December 2015 it was at 6.5%; five months later it was at 11% - an outstanding achievement in such a short period of time.[198] The *return on investment* (ROI) from marketing communications was exceptional, but for business reasons the specific ROI facts are not available for publication; however, the market share figure (11%) is testament to its success.

FIGURE 12.7: ORCHARD THIEVES 48-SHEET POSTER

The success of this launch was not just in the product; the message needed to engage the consumer in exceptionally high numbers and convince the trade to get behind it. The marketing programme was the difference.

Orchard Thieves achieved 11% market share in just over a year – five times the target set for the brand

Agencies: Rothco, Guns or Knives, Starcom and Thinkhouse
Client: HEINEKEN Ireland (Fiona Curtin & Gemma Adams)

198 Rothco and Starcom Ireland, *Orchard Thieves: Thieving the Spotlight*, pg 164.

TEN THINGS TO REMEMBER

WE HAVE COVERED MANY ASPECTS OF MARKETING IN THIS BOOK. WE HAVE IDENTIFIED NUMEROUS PROOF POINTS THAT DEMONSTRATE THE EFFECTIVENESS OF THIS DISCIPLINE, AND WE HAVE HIGHLIGHTED SEVERAL FACTORS THAT AFFECT THE GROWTH AND PROFITABILITY OF BRANDS.

TO CLOSE, WE HAVE PICKED WHAT WE BELIEVE ARE THE TEN MOST IMPORTANT TRUTHS TO REMEMBER.

Marketing generates substantial growth for national economies and businesses

Advertising is extremely important for economic activity; it provides jobs, promotes competition, helps innovation, leads to lower prices and boosts growth in an unambiguously positive way. It is a matter of empirical fact that advertising and national economies are positively correlated to a large degree.

McKinsey found that advertising fuelled about 15% of growth for the major G20 economies between 2001 and 2010.[199] Deloitte calculated that, on average, £1 invested in advertising generates £6 for the UK economy[200]; €1 invested in Ireland generates €5.7 for the Irish economy;[201] $1 generates $3 in the Australian economy[202] and €1 invested in advertising generates €5 in the Belgian economy.[203]

However, we need to be cautious about the use of 'multipliers' and recognise the limitations of current theory and data with regard to macroeconomics.

There is no debate regarding the multipliers reported in the microeconomic world of individual brands, where causation can be clearly proven. Analysis conducted by Core in Ireland, found that €1 invested in advertising typically delivers a revenue return of €8.26 and a net return on investment of €5.44 for brands.[204]

See Chapter 1.8 and Chapter 4 for more.

199 Spittaels and Bughin, *Advertising as an Economic-Growth Engine*, pg 44.
200 Advertising Association and Deloitte, *Advertising Pays (UK)*, pg 48.
201 Deloitte, *Advertising: An Engine for Economic Growth*, pg 10.
202 Deloitte Access Economics, *Advertising Pays (Australia)*, pg 48.
203 Deloitte et al., *Advertising Pays (Belgium)*, pg 48.
204 Core, *Core Meta-Analysis*, pg 76.

Creativity has a profound and quantifiable influence on marketing effectiveness

The value of creativity is proven and quantifiable. Of all the factors that are within the marketer's sphere of influence, this is the most important by far. The choices made in relation to investment in creativity have a massive impact on the growth in profitability of brands.

Creatively-awarded campaigns are six times more efficient than non-awarded campaigns in growing market share.[205] A multiple of six is impressive, but it has declined from a staggering 12.4 in the decade leading up to the financial crisis that gripped the world in 2008.[206] During the recession years that followed, there has been a significant move towards short-termism in marketing, coupled with a decline in marketing communications investment levels. These factors have been directly responsible for halving the effectiveness of creativity in advertising.

See Chapter 11 for more.

[205] Field, *Selling Creativity Short*, pg 11.
[206] Field, *The Link Between Creativity and Effectiveness*, pg 70.

Recruiting new customers is more profitable than trying to increase frequency of purchase. Compelling evidence supports the contention that loyalty programmes have little effect and when they work, they do so by mainly recruiting new customers, not by reducing churn or by extracting more value from existing ones.[207]

Marketers should advertise to everyone in the market for their product, rather than focusing on a small segmented audience. Potential gains from customer acquisition dwarf the potential gains from retention.[208] Loyalty strategies can produce cost-effective short-term activation effects, but the true cost of this is long-term ineffectiveness.[209]

See Chapter 10 for more.

Penetration is more effective than brand loyalty in building growth and profitability

[207] Binet and Field, *Marketing in the Era of Accountability*, pg 12.
[208] Sharp, *How Brands Grow*, pg 137.
[209] Field, *Selling Creativity Short*, pg 11.

The size of a brand has a major impact on the efficiency and effectiveness of marketing communications. Large brands have inherent advantages over smaller brands; they have higher penetration, better distribution, stronger range and pricing strategies that help to maintain and increase share.

Brands with market shares of over 10% achieve circa two and a half times the level of share growth, for each point of *extra share of voice (ESOV)*, as compared with brands that have market shares of under 10%.[210] Therefore, smaller brands need to over invest, relative to their market share, to compete effectively. They must also devise campaigns with above average effectiveness (from a creative standpoint) to drive growth.

See Chapter 7 for more.

Brand size has a significant influence on marketing effectiveness

4

[210] Nielsen and IPA, *How Share of Voice Wins Market Share*, pg 12.

Short-term marketing initiatives are less effective than long-term campaigns in building growth and profitability

Short-term marketing is on the rise and it is damaging the profitability of marketing. This shift has been caused by recession-driven urgency, in businesses, to build immediate sales and a belief among senior management that this will be achieved through short-term tactics (rather than long-term brand-building strategies). However, long-term campaigns (those that are evaluated over periods of longer than six months) are around three times more efficient than short-term campaigns.[211] Short-term initiatives are, in fact, more effective at driving transient sales effects, but they deliver weak long-term growth. Businesses need to employ both techniques, but in the correct proportion.

See Chapter 8 for more.

211 Field, *Selling Creativity Short*, pg 11.

Emotional campaigns produce considerably more powerful long-term business effects than rational campaigns

Emotionally-based campaigns outperform rationally-based campaigns on every business measure; they are significantly more profitable, they are better at generating awareness, they are stronger at creating differentiation and they form more durable memories of brands in consumers' minds.[212]

Rational campaigns do enjoy an advantage in relation to short-term direct effects, but this advantage is temporary. Marketers should adopt a carefully balanced approach that drives both long-term brand preference (through emotion) and short-term sales (through rational messaging).

See Chapter 9 for more.

212 Binet and Field, *Marketing in the Era of Accountability*, pg 12.

Points five and six above are interwoven; emotional techniques tend to be employed in long-term brand marketing programmes and rational techniques are prevalent in short-term sales activation campaigns. They both have their place, but over/underinvesting in one or the other will damage the growth of a brand.

On average, marketers should spend 60% of their budget on brand-building activity (long-term, broad reach, emotional) and 40% on sales activation (short-term, tightly targeted and information rich), to achieve maximum efficiency and maximum effectiveness.[213]

See Chapter 8 for more.

Marketers need to strike the optimum balance between brand building and activation spends

[213] Binet and Field, *Marketing in the Era of Accountability*, pg 12.

Successful owned and earned media strategies are dependent on paid media

Brands using paid media typically grow three times faster than those that just rely on owned and earned media. However, paid media will only be at their most effective when combined with strong earned and owned strands. Owned media typically increase the effectiveness of a paid campaign by 13%, while adding earned media causes an increase of 26%.[214] However, very few campaigns generate strong effects without having paid media in place.

See Chapter 12 for more.

[214] Clift, *Marketing in the Digital Age*, pg 110.

Many methods are used to set budgets for marketing communications, but very few are scientific. In addition, they are usually not geared to identify the optimum level of investment for the specific business challenge being faced.

Econometrics is the gold standard in most cases, because it is bespoke to the brand in question and it uses systematic modelling to understand how all key variables impact sales. It generates response curves, which enable practitioners to forecast revenue and profit for different levels of investment in marketing communications. This, in turn, drives an optimisation tool, which calculates the impact of different budget levels and media combinations to arrive at the ideal level of investment for the campaign in question.

Another reliable method is based on the relationship between *share of voice* (SOV) and *share of market* (SOM). Research has proven that when a brand's SOV is greater than its SOM, it is more likely to gain market share. The crucial measure of this phenomenon is *extra share of voice* (ESOV). A useful rule of thumb is that for every ten points of ESOV a brand should expect to gain one percentage point of extra market share growth across a year. However, this is just a starting point; many factors including brand size, market category, product life stage and campaign quality impact this relationship.

See Chapter 7 for more.

To understand how much to invest, scientific budget-setting techniques must be used

A commitment to marketing analytics significantly improves return on investment

Marketing analytics is the measurement and optimisation of marketing activities. It is important to continually analyse all marketing activity in order to grow the effectiveness of campaigns on a compound basis. Marketers must create a measurement culture within their organisations and every brand should budget for it.

Investment in marketing analytics gives practitioners ongoing evidence-based guidance on how to 'course correct' their plans to build market share growth. Failing to invest in scientific analysis and modelling reduces brand profitability.

The benefits can be enormous; an integrated analytics approach can free up between 15% and 20% of marketing spending.[215]

See Chapter 6 for more.

[215] Bhandari et al., *Using Marketing Analytics to Drive Superior Growth*, pg 96.

BIBLIOGRAPHY

Account Planning Group. (See www.apg.org.uk for more)

adam&eveDDB London. *John Lewis: Monty's Christmas*. Warc. 2016.

Advertising Association and Deloitte. *Advertising Pays: How Advertising Fuels the UK Economy*. January 2013.

Advertising Association and Deloitte. *Advertising Pays 2: How Advertising Can Unlock UK Growth Potential*. January 2014.

AECOM. *The Economic Impact of Advertising in Ireland*. Association of Advertisers in Ireland (AAI). May 2012.

Akerlof, George A. and Shiller, Robert J. *Phishing for Phools: The Economics of Manipulation and Deception*. US: Princeton University Press. 2015.

Albert, Alexandra and Reid, Benjamin. *The Contribution of the Advertising Industry to the UK Economy*. Creative Industries and Credos. November 2011.

Arrow, Kenneth J. and Nerlove, Marc. *Optimal Advertising Policy Under Dynamic Conditions*. Economica, 29(114). 1962.

Ashley, Richard; Granger, Clive W. J.; and Schmalensee, Richard. *Advertising and Aggregate Consumption: An Analysis of Causality*. Econometrica, 48(5). 1980.

Austin, Anne; Barnard, Johnathan; and Hutcheon, Nicola. *Zenith Advertising Expenditure Forecast*. December 2016.

Bagwell, Kyle. *The Economic Analysis of Advertising*. US: Columbia University Department of Economics, Discussion Paper Series (01). August 2005.

Barton, Dominic and Wiseman, Mark. *Focusing Capital on the Long Term.* Harvard Business Review. January - February 2014.

Batini, Nicoletta; Eyraud, Luc; and Weber, Anke. *A Simple Method to Compute Fiscal Multipliers.* IMF Working Paper, 14/93. June 2014.

Bhandari, Rishi; Singer, Marc; and Van Der Scheer, Hiek. *Using Marketing Analytics to Drive Superior Growth*. McKinsey & Company. June 2014.

Binet, Les et al. *The Gift That Keeps on Giving: John Lewis Christmas Advertising, 2012-2015*. Warc. 2016.

Binet, Les and Field, Peter. *Marketing in the Digital Age*. UK: Institute of Practitioners in Advertising (IPA). October 2016.

Binet, Les and Field, Peter. *Marketing in the Era of Accountability*. UK: Institute of Practitioners in Advertising (IPA) and Warc. 2007.

Binet, Les and Field, Peter. *The Long and the Short of it: Balancing Short and Long-Term Marketing Strategies*. UK: Institute of Practitioners in Advertising (IPA). 2013.

Bittlingmayer, George. *Advertising*. The Concise Encyclopaedia of Economics: Library of Economics and Liberty. 2008.

Borden, Neil H. *The Economic Effects of Advertising*. US: Richard D. Irwin Inc. 1942.

Broadbent, Simon. *The Advertising Budget: The Advertiser's Guide to Budget Determination*. McGraw-Hill. 1989.

Buck, Stephan. *The True Cost of Cutting Ad-Spend*. Warc. 2001.

Burke-Kennedy, Eoin. *Ad Man Sutherland Brings His Roadshow to Kilkenomics*. Irish Times. November 2015.

Burrows, Peter. *Back to the Future at Apple*. Bloomberg. May 1998.

Cannes Lions Archive. (See www.canneslionsarchive.com for more)

Cavenaile, Laurent and Roldan, Pau. *Advertising, Innovation and Economic Growth*. US: New York University. 2016.

Cawley Nea\TBWA and Carat. *HSE QUIT 2.* ADFX Databank. 2014.

Cawley Nea\TBWA and Mediavest. *HSE QUIT*. ADFX Databank. 2012.

Chamberlin, Edward. *The Theory of Monopolistic Competition: A Re-orientation of the Theory of Value*. US: Harvard University Press. 1933.

Clift, Joseph. *Marketing in the Digital Age: Binet and Field on How Media Choices Impact Effectiveness*. Warc. 2016.

Core. *Core Meta-Analysis*. 2016.

Coveney, Patrick. *The Advertising Evangelist*. Business & Finance CEO 100 edition. October 2016.

Cullen, Paul. *Irish Smoking Rates Falling Fastest in EU, Says Survey*. The Irish Times. 2015.

Cyron, Gerald. *Coca-Cola: Share a Coke (Australia)*. Warc. 2012.

Deloitte. *Advertising: An Engine for Economic Growth*. October 2013.

Deloitte and Radd voor de Reclame/Conseil de la Publicité. *Advertising Pays: The Impact of Advertising on the Belgian Economy*. 2015.

Department of the Environment. *Northern Ireland Seatbelt Survey*. 2000.

Drucker, Peter F. *Post Capitalist Society*. Harper Information. 1993.

Econsultancy and Oracle Marketing Cloud. *Marketers in the Boardroom*. November 2015.

Effie Worldwide. (See www.effie.org for more)

Ehrenberg, Andrew S. C. *Repetitive Advertising and the Consumer*. Journal of Advertising Research, 40(6). 2000.

Ehrenberg, Andrew S. C.; Goodhardt, Gerald G.; and Barwise, Patrick. *Double Jeopardy Revisited*. Journal of Marketing, 54(3). 1990.

Ehrenberg, Andrew S. C.; Uncles, Mark D.; and Goodhardt, Gerald G. *Understanding Brand Performance Measures: Using Dirichlet Benchmarks*. Journal of Business Research, 57(12). 2004.

Ekelund, Robert B. and Gramm, William P. *A Reconsideration of Advertising Expenditures, Aggregate Demand and Economic Stabilisation*. Quarterly Review of Economics and Business, 9 (Summer). 1969.

Esterel, Mike. *'Share a Coke' Credited with a Pop in Sales*. The Wall Street Journal. 2014.

Fanning, John. *I Must Be Talking to My Friends*. Institute of Advertising Practitioners in Ireland (IAPI) and Television Audience Measurement Ireland (TAM Ireland). 2015.

Farris, Paul W.; Hanssens, Dominique M.; Lenskold, James, D.; and Reibstein, David J. *Marketing Return on Investment: Seeking Clarity for Concept and Measurement*. Applied Marketing Analytics, 1(3). 2015.

Field, Peter. *Selling Creativity Short*. UK: Institute of Practitioners in Advertising (IPA) and Thinkbox. 2016.

Field, Peter. *The Link Between Creativity and Effectiveness*. UK: Institute of Practitioners in Advertising (IPA). 2010.

Field, Peter. *The Link Between Creativity and Effectiveness (Update)*. UK: Institute of Practitioners in Advertising (IPA). 2011.

Forbes. *The World's Most Valuable Brands*. 2017.

Forsman & Bodenfors. *Volvo Trucks: Live Test Series*. Warc. 2015.

Galton, Francis. *Hereditary Genius: An Inquiry into its Laws and Consequences*. Macmillan, 1869.

Golding, David et al. *John Lewis: Making the Nation Cry... and Buy*. Warc. 2012.

Hand, Karen and McGrath, Jill. *A Line in the Sand*. Institute of Advertising Practitioners in Ireland (IAPI) and Television Audience Measurement Ireland (TAM Ireland). 2015.

Heath, Robert and Feldwick, Paul. *50 Years Using the Wrong Model of TV Advertising*. International Journal of Market Research, 50(1). 2008.

Heath, Robert. *TV Strategy: The Art of Subconscious Seduction*. Admap. 2014.

Hoffman, Bob. *The Mass Marketing Zombie*. The Ad Contrarian. February 2012.

HSE. *Smoking - The Facts*. Ireland: Health Service Executive. 2016.

Hupp, Oliver. *Loyalty is the Key Driver of Brand Growth*. Admap. September 2016.

Hurman, James. *The Case for Creativity*. New Zealand: AUT Media. 2011.

IAPI ADFX Databank. (See www.adfx.ie/databank for more).

IHS (Economics and Country Risk). *Economic Impact of Advertising in the United States*. The Advertising Coalition. March 2015.

IHS (Global Insight). *The Economic Impact of Advertising Expenditures in the Unites States.* The Advertising Coalition. August 2010.

IHS (Global Insight). *The Economic Impact of Advertising Expenditures in the United States, 2012-2017.* The Advertising Coalition. January 2014.

IPA. *Advertising in a Downturn: A Report of Key Findings from an IPA Seminar.* UK: Institute of Practitioners in Advertising (IPA). March 2008.

IPA Effectiveness Hub. (See www.ipa.co.uk/effectiveness/case-studies for more).

Iyer, Byravee. *Volvo Insiders on Creating, and Following up on, the 'Epic Split'.* Campaign Asia. September 2014.

Jones, John P. *Ad Spending: Maintaining Market Share.* Harvard Business Review, 68(1). 1990.

Kantar Millward Brown. *BrandZ™ Top 100 Most Valuable Global Brands (10th Anniversary Edition).* 2015.

Kaplan, Robert S. and Shocker, Allan D. *Discount Effects on Media Plans.* Journal of Advertising Research, 11(3). 1971.

Lyle, David, et al. Department of the Environment (NI) and Road Safety Authority (ROI) - *The longer-term effects of seatbelt advertising 2001–2007.* Warc. 2008.

McGraw-Hill Research. *Laboratory of Advertising Performance Report 5262.* US: McGraw-Hill. 1986.

Mendoza, Luis. *Coca-Cola: Share a Coke (US).* Warc. 2015.

Mirzaei, Abas et al. *Assessing Ad-Spend Patterns to Predict Brand Health: A Model for Advertisers to Determine Future Advertising-Budgeting Strategies.* Journal of Advertising Research, 56(2). April 2016.

Nayaradou, Maximilien. *Advertising and Economic Growth*. World Federation of Advertisers. 2006.

Nicosia, Franco M. and Jacobson, Robert. *Advertising and Public Policy: The Macroeconomic Effects of Advertising*. Journal of Marketing Research, 18(1). 1981.

Nielsen and IPA. *How Share of Voice Wins Market Share*. UK: Institute of Practitioners in Advertising (IPA) and Nielsen Analytic Consulting. 2009.

Nielsen. *Global Trust in Advertising: Winning Strategies for an Evolving Media Landscape*. 2015.

Ogilvy & Mather Bogotá. *Coca-Cola: The Gift Bottle*. Warc. 2016.

Peckham, James O. *The Wheel of Marketing*. 1973.

Philip, Matthew; Weavers, Helen; Adams, Paddy; Clear, Caroline; Pearson, Tim; Bratt, David; Marwaha, Preety; Dias, Sam; Orton, Tim. *Should've Gone to Specsavers: A Far-Sighted View of Advertising's Role in Building a Business Over 30 Years*. Warc. 2014.

Rauch, Ferdinand. *Advertising and Consumer Prices*. VOX (CEPR Policy Portal). November 2012.

Rauch, Ferdinand. *Advertising Expenditure and Consumer Prices*. UK: Centre for Economic Performance (CEP) Discussion Paper 1073. August 2011.

Rothco and Starcom Ireland. *Orchard Thieves: Thieving the Spotlight*. Warc. 2016.

RSA. *Seatbelt Observational Study*. Ireland: Road Safety Authority. 1999.

Rust, Roland T.; Ambier, Tim.; Carpenter, Gregory S.; Kumar, V.; and Srivastava, Rajendra K. *Measuring Marketing Productivity: Current Knowledge and Future Direction*. Journal of Marketing, 68(4). 2004.

Sharp, Byron and Newstead, Kate. *Loyalty is Not the Holy Grail*. Admap. 2010.

Sharp, Byron. *How Brands Grow: What Marketers Don't Know*. Oxford University Press. 2010.

Sharp, Byron. *Marketing Science Commentary*. September 2016.

Smith, Noah. *Economics Has a Math Problem*. Bloomberg. September 2015.

Spittaels, Steven and Bughin, Jacques. *Advertising as an Economic-Growth Engine*. McKinsey & Company. March 2012.

Steiner, Peter O. and Dorfman, Robert. *Optimal Advertising and Optimal Quality*. American Economic Review, 44(5). 1954.

Stigler, George and Arrow, Kenneth J. *Miscellaneous Revenue Issues*. US: Government Printing Office. 1993.

Sutherland, Rory. *Branding Heterodox Economics*. Synthesis. November 2012.

Tabarrok, Alex. *A Phool and His Money: Review of Phishing for Phools*. The New Rambler. 2015.

Taylor, Timothy. *The Case For and Against Advertising*. Conversable Economist. November 2012.

The Best of Global Digital Marketing. *Case Study: Volvo Trucks Live Test Series*. 2016.

The Coca-Cola Company. *Annual Report (Form 10K)*. US: The Coca-Cola Company. 2015.

The Coca-Cola Company. *Who We Are*. Infograph. 2017.

The Investment Association UK. *Public Position Statement: Quarterly Reporting and Quarterly Earnings Guidance.* November 2016.

Verdon, W. A.; McConnell, C. R.; and Roesler, T. W. *Advertising Expenditures as an Economic Stabiliser 1945-1964*. Quarterly Review of Economics and Business, 8 (Summer). 1969.

Volvo Group. *The Volvo Group Annual and Sustainability Report*. 2015.

Warc. (See www.warc.com for more)

Warc. *What We Know About Brand Loyalty.* Warc Best Practice. October 2016.

Whitler, Kimberly A. *Why Few Marketers are Invited to Join Boards of Directors*. Forbes. January 2016.

Printed in Great Britain
by Amazon